For Christine

Virtue does not come from money,
but money comes from virtue.
                                    Plato

It really is an exciting time –
so exciting that people are
completely confused.
Mikhail Gorbachev (on the 1990s)

Contents

ETHICAL BANKING

Also by James J. Lynch

A MANPOWER DEVELOPMENT SYSTEM
AIRLINE ORGANISATION
MAKING MANPOWER EFFECTIVE
MAKING MANPOWER MORE EFFECTIVE
THE PEOPLE/POWER GAP

Ethical Banking

Surviving in an Age of Default

James J. Lynch

St. Martin's Press   New York

332.1068
L 98 e

All rights reserved. For information, write:
Scholarly and Reference Division,
St. Martin's Press, Inc., 175 Fifth Avenue,
New York, N.Y. 10010

First published in the United States of America in 1991

Printed in Hong Kong

ISBN 0–312–06201–X

Library of Congress Cataloging-in-Publication Data
Lynch, James J.
Ethical banking: surviving in an age of default / James J.
Lynch.
p.   cm.
Includes bibliographical references and index.
ISBN 0–312–06201–X
1. Banks and banking — Moral and ethical aspects.   2. Customer
service.   I. Title.
HG1573.L96   1991
332.1'068'8—dc20   91–12213
                                                    CIP

viii   *Contents*

Contents

*Virtue does not come from money,
but money comes from virtue.*
Plato

*It really is an exciting time –
so exciting that people are
completely confused.*
Mikhail Gorbachev (on the 1990s)

For Christine

PART II   DISCUSSION EXERCISES AND PROBLEMS

Contents   xi

List of Tables and Figures

Tables

Figures

Preface

For the past ten years I have worked closely with banks and other financial institutions in a number of countries as an adviser on issues of management development and service quality. That experience has made me aware of the many pressures which are affecting banks, their managers, staff and customers. Few, if any, other industries have had to cope with such a welter of changes in technology, legislation, customer needs and expectations; change will be a continuing challenge for any involved in banking and financial services. Now a new cancer is spreading through all areas of banking – the cancer of 'default respectability'.

Starting in the early 1980s, default of sovereign debt began to increase. Nations failed to meet their obligations and survived as banks agreed to reschedule and refinance their debts. Later in the decade Citicorp set a trend by 'writing off' hundreds of millions of dollars in sovereign debt. This virtually coincided with the collapse of the Stock Market in 1987 and subsequent failure of major companies and, in the United States, savings and loans institutions. When 'banks' default on their customers, customers default on banks.

Bankruptcy, liquidation, growing arrears in mortgage and other loan repayments have reached epidemic proportions. What was once perceived as the last resort of the scoundrel has begun to gain social acceptance, hence my phrase 'default respectability'.

Banks and other financial institutions will only be able to manage unethical behaviour of customers effectively if they themselves are squeaky clean. More efficient credit controls, stricter auditing, better training in risk management, all have a part to play. But in the end behaviour breeds behaviour, be it between individuals or corporations.

Any perceived unethical behaviour by a bank will breed unethical behaviour by its customers.

Money is the life-blood of banking, service is the heart, ethics the soul. Although the shape of the corporate body of a bank may change, these three remain the life-force of banking. This book focuses on the heart and soul of banking; customer care without ethics is a cynical, sterile exercise. In this world of constant change ethical banking is the cutting-edge of customer care; it restores the concept of reciprocal obligation of banker and customer which is the fulcrum on which the survival of banking depends.

The title *Ethical Banking* is not meant to imply that banking is not 'ethical'; rather, it highlights the need for both bankers and customers to recognise that providing ethical banking is no easy task – both parties have a role to play. For too long the subject has been hidden under a veil of ill-conceived decency or trendily dressed in terms of charitable works and ecological awareness. It is time to rend the veil and discard the trendy suit.

Ethical Banking is about the conventions which govern relationships between one individual (the 'banker') and another (the 'customer'). Each has his or her own needs and expectations. This book is about how to satisfy the interests of both parties in a manner which they, and society would agree is ethical. By this means, 'default respectability' will fail to secure ground to become a scourge of bank managers.

In the book I have drawn on my experience of conducting literally hundreds of workshops and other training events for bankers in Britain, Ireland and the USA. A period as the first Head of Management Training for the Barclays Group provided an extremely useful insight into the myriad of problems faced by bank staff and their determination to resolve them ethically. More recently my work with other financial services has enabled me to witness banks seeking to transform their ethical aspirations into a day-to-day reality.

I hope that all banks and financial institutions will find in these pages an echo of problems they are facing and a guide to resolving them in a manner which will stamp the 1990s as the decade of ethical banking rather than the age of default.

Lions Green   JAMES J. LYNCH
East Sussex

Note: For details of consultancy and training services on ethical banking please contact:

Service Excellence Associates
Lions Green House
Lions Green
Heathfield
East Sussex TN21 OPJ

Tel. 04353 2599
Fax. 04353 2599

Part I

The Essentials of Ethical Banking

1 The Need to Define Ethical Banking

1.1 INTRODUCTION

Ethical banking is about corporate living, not corporate giving, about investing time in ethical practices rather than money in 'ethical' funds. Today's bankers need to adapt the ethical traditions of the past to the new demands of the future. This book shows how this can be done.

Since its earliest beginnings banking has been perceived as a business which depends on mutual trust and personal integrity. Through the centuries there have been breaches of that trust and lapses of integrity by both bankers and their clients. The rarity of these has led them to be causes for scandal which, on occasion, have overshadowed the normal high standards of banking.

The 1980s witnessed an eruption of scandals from Wall Street to the City of London, from tiny Liechtenstein to minuscule Gibraltar. Institutions whose names were synonymous with high moral tone suddenly sounded discordant notes which jarred their multinational clients and frightened the customer in the high street. Why this sudden shift in the paradigm of probity which had underpinned banking for decades? Even more important, what action is needed to stop the rot; to re-establish trust; to reinforce the traditional values of banking to which the vast majority of banks and their staffs have always subscribed?

This book seeks to answer these questions, first, by identifying the forces which are influencing ethical banking and then showing how to use many of these to shape behaviour and implement practices which will not simply bring back into play the standards of the past, but will create the conditions necessary for banking and financial services to play a leading role in creating a moral climate from which all – customers, shareholders and employees – will benefit in the 1990s and beyond.

1.2 THE FORCES SHAPING ETHICAL STANDARDS IN BANKING

For most of this century banking has changed little in Britain in terms of market forces. The mergers of the late nineteenth century which gave rise to the major clearing banks resulted in at least one branch of a large, reliable bank in every town and in most hamlets. Personal customers were drawn mainly from the middle classes. (The aristocracy used merchant banks; the working classes used the Post Office, Trustee Savings Bank and regional banks such as the Yorkshire Penny Bank.)

In the 'good old days' up to the 1950s, bank managers knew most of their personal customers, many of them on intimate social terms; they shared their values and safeguarded their interests. Many managers stayed at the same branch for years, becoming part of the social fabric. The banks formed a cosy cartel which agreed rates to be charged for borrowing, to be paid for investing. For much of the time the rates remained constant. It was a world of stability, integrity, consistency. Yet it was also a world in which banks lived a big lie. They convinced their customers that banking was free; they led their managers to believe that banking was not a business, subject to market forces, but was, in a sense, a social institution somewhat like the Church of England of old, a contributor to well-being which, while open to all, preferred to attract a decent class of people who would abide by the rules.

Banks did not set out deliberately to deceive their customers, rather their attitude was one of paternalism, not wanting to confuse the children with matters they believed were beyond their ken.

The 1960s witnessed a change in the structure of banking with the merger of the National Provincial and Westminster Banks and, on a smaller scale, Barclays and Martins Banks. These monoliths would soon become hungry for business which would sustain their over-branched, overmanned organisations since staff involved in the mergers were assured of continued employment. Competitive pressures would eventually crack the cartel and put some traditional banking values under strain.

Another break with tradition towards the end of the 1960s was the decision by Barclays to copy Bank of America and venture into the new world of credit cards. With the creation of Barclaycard came undreamt of profit opportunities and unforeseen threats – the impact of the computer and the need to recruit a new breed of employees, computer specialists who did not necessarily share traditional bank values.

At one fell swoop, Barclays sought to create a new mass financial service – Barclaycard – and to dominate the market by an unprecedented investment in technology. The bank managed to keep its rivals at bay for almost seven years when the other clearers linked together to create Access. Unwittingly, these initiatives of the late 1960s and early 1970s would give rise to two of the forces which would shape ethical banking in the 1980s and will continue to do so in the foreseeable future.

The mass market for a single product called for a massive dependency on automation. More and more customers would feel that they had a technological relationship with their bank. At the mercy of the inanimate computer, the tradition of 'customer loyalty' was being eroded; the scope for malpractice through 'computer fraud' was vastly increasing. The second force which Barclaycard would eventually unleash was the 'global product'. By the mid 1980s Barclaycard would be part of the American based Visa, Access would be part of MasterCard. Each of these credit card companies bestrides the globe; each card can be used in many markets where ethical standards vary; each provides new opportunities for fraud. Perhaps even more telling in terms of ethics in banking, customers who felt they had been victimised by credit and other bank card processing, began to distrust the administrative competence of banks and to question their integrity.

In the 1980s, the world of banking and financial services exploded with the Big Bang in London in 1986, but there had been a number of other explosions which had an impact on ethics in banking earlier in the decade.

The soaring rise of oil prices in the mid 1970s resulted in the banks of Iran, Saudi Arabia and the Gulf coming on to the international scene. Unlike the dominant Protestant ethic of Western banks, these Moslem banks based their practices on the Koran. Debarred by the teachings of the Prophet from charging interest, Islamic banks have devised a variety of trading and sharing practices which call for high standards of ethical behaviour by both lender and borrower, although the drop in oil prices and the rise of the Islamic Revolution in Iran have curtailed the influence of Islamic banking in the West. But one has only to look at the increasing numbers of Moslems in Britain and across the world to surmise that the Koran could increasingly become a source for new ethics in banking in the 1990s. This is developed more fully in Chapter 2.

The other major cultural influence on modern banking is the growing power of Japan. Not only does that country account for nine of the ten largest banks in the world, its increasing ownership of financial institutions in the USA and Europe will undoubtedly influence ethics in banking – not necessarily for the better. In the West, Japanese banks have concentrated largely on the corporate sector. They have developed a reputation for adopting a long-term view in considering the plans of clients, but where they are not locked into commercial arrangements they are more ready to withdraw their support from clients in times of crisis than would be the practice of many Western banks, particularly the British and German. Trends in Japanese banking are covered in Chapter 2.

The Single Market of 1992 will witness an increase in the merging of banks from different countries and ethical traditions. Banks will find themselves faced not only with new types of competition but with new types of customers. In the main, these new customers will be more financially sophisticated, consumer rights oriented and less 'loyal' than their forefathers. We shall explore this further in Chapter 5.

Despite the claim of politicians that the changes of the Big Bang of 1986 to the structure of British financial markets were part of a process of 'deregulation', the reality was one of reregulation. New rules and new bodies to enforce them came into play. After five years both the regulators and the regulated are still experiencing difficulties in adjusting to the changes, as we shall see in Chapter 6.

There were several other forces at work in the financial world of the late 1980s which coincided with 'Big Bang' and which have had repercussions on ethics in banking.

Starting in the United States, there was a virtual stampede of mergers and acquisitions across the industrial map. New methods of financing these were devised of which the most notorious was the 'junk bond'. These high interest instruments were built on the somewhat shallow base of the prospective performance of the merged companies. They promised quick profits from the alchemist gold of financial wizardry; their values proved worthless when, like the alchemist gold, they were tested in the cauldron of the market. Of particular significance was the 'Black Monday' of October 1987. On that fateful day, many small investors on both sides of the Atlantic saw the value of their savings fall drastically. In the United States, disillusion with financial institutions was compounded by the failure of many savings and loan companies (building societies) where small investors suffered, while so-called rescuers of these companies prospered.

The claim of Ivan Boesky that 'greed is good' resounded through Wall Street and was carried across the Atlantic. Privatisation in Britain provided huge fees for financiers and public relations companies, massive rises for top executives of the privatised companies, quick profits for millions of small shareholders. Mergers and acquisitions in Britain were not financed by junk bonds but were accompanied by junk ethics. The man and woman in the street read about bribes, fixed markets, success fees, golden welcomes, platinum parachutes. Small companies launched on the Unlisted Securities Market were oversubscribed many times by investors bedazzled more by a barrage of sales propaganda than by the long-term sales potential of those to whom they were entrusting their life savings.

Penalties for making millions through insider dealing were on a par with those for parking illegally. Immunity was granted to financial 'wunderkind' who had accumulated fortunes and lied about their methods. Young people of limited experience were offered six-figure salaries and super cars. Major banks found themselves caught up in the webs of dubious dealings spun by people who believed that their illicit behaviour would merit nothing more than a metaphorical 'slap on the wrist' from the regulators. They found to their surprise that officialdom influenced by public opinion demanded that instead of slapped wrists, heads should roll – still metaphorically speaking, of course.

A factor which throughout the decades had been little more than a diversion to those engaged in banking became an obsession in the 1980s. Competition reared up on all sides and scattered such myths that banks provide current accounts and building societies provide house loans. For a period in the 1980s Barclays Bank became the third largest 'building society' in terms of home loans; building societies set the pace in providing innovative current accounts.

By 1990, the world of banking in Britain, the United States and most of Europe had changed out of recognition from ten years previously. Automation has greatly increased the speed of processing data, automated teller machines provide constant access to cash and account details. Competition has extended the range of products and services available from staff who have undergone training in 'customer care'. Legislation has safeguarded the rights of consumers in wide areas of financial dealings and ensures that customers are better informed about interest rates, fees and commission standards.

Much has improved in banking, but the very forces which have shaped the modern edifice of financial services have dented the keystone – ethical banking. The new environment calls for new behaviour. Such behaviour must enable bankers to perform their role in a manner which conforms to high standards of professional probity while achieving the business goals of their bank in an acutely competitive environment. The conforming, unquestioning, cautious banker of old needs to give way to a person true to himself, true to his customers and true to his bank – the ethical banker.

Ethics define a code of conduct which is accepted by the parties involved as being in accord with the highest moral standards of the society of which they are part.

As the world of banking changes, so it is necessary to review and where necessary revise the ethical codes which govern our actions.

1.3 NEW PRESSURES ON BANKERS

We will discuss in this book the five major forces which are creating the need for defining more explicitly what is meant by ethical banking:

(1) Consumer-oriented laws
(2) Consumer awareness
(3) Competition
(4) Performance-related payment
(5) Assertive employees

Consumer-oriented laws cover all industries but, as we shall see in Chapter 6, banking has more than its fair share. Unfortunately, the more laws that exist the greater the temptation to circumvent them. There is no virtue in complying with the law, that is the least that the State expects. Virtue comes from going beyond the requirements of the law in providing service to a fellow being; it also comes from voluntarily pre-empting the need for law by undertaking ethical action.

Consumers are more aware of their rights than ever before. This is due in part to the mass media, but also to a realisation that there is such a phenomenon as 'customer power'. Whether it be demanding a return to the shelves of their favourite 'Coca-cola', the closure of nuclear energy plants, or the retention of handwritten bank deposit books, customers across the world are exercising their power.

In relation to banking, customers are voicing their needs in five simple phrases. They want financial services:

(1) any time;
(2) any place;
(3) right first time;
(4) no paper;
(5) just for me.

Customers want easy access to details of their financial affairs any time in twenty-four hours. They do not want to travel any great distance to receive financial advice. Whether it is advice or a statement of their account, they expect it to be accurate. As far as possible, they want the minimum of forms and other paperwork in any transaction. Finally, they want the 'personal touch'.

Satisfying these wants can pose some ethical dilemmas for any banker since he is not alone in responding to them. Political, economic and technological changes have in a sense transformed the 'local bank' to the 'global bank'. Whether by telephone, satellite or courier mail, the distant competitor can become the local rival. This puts severe strains on the local branch manager.

At least part of the strain arises from new payment systems which are based on achieving sales targets rather than years of service. Today, bank managers are in a double change loop; expected to change their behaviour while managing the changes affecting staff and customers.

Bank staff, in common with better educated employees everywhere, are becoming more assertive, more questioning, less willing to have ethical codes imposed on them without justification. They need help in responding to the changes that affect their managers. They need guidance in resolving ethical dilemmas.

1.4 A NEW ROLE FOR BANKERS

Decisions on creditworthiness are increasingly being made by 'computer models'. Opportunities for investment are similar between companies. Money transmission is less relevant in an age of credit cards and automated teller machines (ATMs). The role of the banker is changing from one of decision to one of counselling.

What will keep the role alive is the ability to judge and advise within an acceptable ethical framework. Computers are incapable of ethical judgement; man is not.

The role of the bank manager is increasingly becoming one of

helping customers to make the best use of their human potential by
lending them the necessary finance, and of their achievements by
providing opportunities to invest in their savings. As their role is
transformed, bankers need to have a framework for determining
their ethical behaviour.

1.5   ETHICAL PROBLEMS

This book does not claim to teach ethics in the sense that bookkeep-
ing or a language can be taught. It will, however, help you to become
more ethically aware in handling day to day problems. Twenty-three
problems, individual and group exercises will provide you with con-
crete means of discussing ethical issues with your colleagues. Background commentaries on developments in banking which are raising
ethical issues will enable you to put your role and your bank in
context. You will be able to compare the responses of other banks to
problems which you share.

   Above all, you will be provided with five canons of ethical banking
and shown how to apply these to situations which, while you may not
be able to resolve them to everyone's satisfaction, will leave you with
a clear conscience and a reputation for ethical banking.

2 The Future Shape of Ethical Banking

2.1 INTRODUCTION

The 1990s will witness changes in the four major geopolitical banking areas of the world – Europe, the United States, Japan and the Middle East. Some of these changes will be interactive, cutting across national and international boundaries to form a lattice-like network of cultural and financial relationships. These relationships will influence ethical codes and behaviour by bringing into play new mixtures of ethical traditions which hitherto have operated separately in their local markets.

European and US banks have followed the Hellenic and Judaeo-Christian philosophies with emphasis on the golden rule, 'Do unto others as you would have them do unto you'. In the United States, banks in this century have been more circumscribed by law than has been the situation, until recently, in Europe. This reliance on the rule of law will become more marked but with a significant change of emphasis. Whereas since the 1930s US banking law has been primarily concerned with preventing fraud and safeguarding the savings of investors, the future trend will be to enforce banks to contribute to solving community problems. In ethical terms, the move is away from 'You can't do this' to 'You must do that'.

For example, under US Federal law, those regulators responsible for approving bank mergers have a duty to ensure that banks lend in all areas, including poor ones, where their depositors live. The existence of this law was used by pressure groups in California, the 'Greenliners', to influence the policies of Japanese banks which now have a dominant role in that state. One of the problems facing Japanese banks in the United States has been a lack of experience in dealing with ethnic groups in a sensitive manner. This can result in perceptions of 'unethical' behaviour on the part of the Japanese, and sometimes oversensitivity to pressure groups. When California First (Japanese owned) bought Union Bank, the latter invested $84 million in poor neighbourhoods due, it is claimed, to the 'Greenliners'. (The name 'Greenliners' was coined to counteract the practice of

11

some US banks which 'redline' certain neighbourhoods which they consider too risky for loans.)

This one example reflects some of the forces at work in shaping ethical banking – legislation, social pressures, changes in ownership. There are others as we shall see in this chapter.

2.2   TRENDS IN EUROPEAN BANKING

The major factors shaping the European banking scene in the 1990s are:

(1) the unification of Germany;
(2) the Single European Market from 1992;
(3) the rebirth of East European banking.

The unification of Germany will be the single greatest force on ethical banking in Europe because it will lead to the expansion of the concept of the 'universal bank', not only in the new Germany but in both a EEC and the countries of Eastern Europe.

The 'universal bank' combines traditional banking with investment banking (corporate finance, stockbroking, dealing, etc.). A distinctive characteristic in contrast to British and US banks is that the universal banks own large stakes in their industrial clients; they are involved in the direction and operation of the companies in which they have a stake. Deutsche Bank is the largest 'universal bank'.

A study published by the Centre for European Policy Studies in Brussels, in 1990, sought to cast doubts on the spread of the universal bank concept. It argued that it is a phenomenon specific in time and place to the rebuilding of post-war Germany. At the time the report was prepared Germany was still totally divided and its Eastern neighbours were under Communist rule. Now all that has changed.

The arguments against universal banks are:

(1) They have not benefited from economies of scale.
(2) They are slow to react and can be outmatched in performance by small 'boutique banks'.
(3) They are at risk if one of their major industrial investments goes wrong.
(4) There can be conflicts of interest between the roles of lender and investor to the same company.

(5) There is a danger of concentration of power since universal banks dominate the credit system and investment market.

Against these economic arguments the significance of universal banks for ethical banking is that they perform a 'social' role in their home market. By being willing to forgo part of their profit in the long-term interests of their clients or to further a particular project, they can help safeguard the interests of the economy as a whole. Furthermore, they can influence the ethical behaviour of clients in whom they have a stake. This means that they must be clear about their own ethical values and standards.

Universal banking was born in a post-war era of reconstruction in Germany. With all its faults it has contributed to the development of Europe's strongest economy. There can be little doubt that universal banking will prosper in the post-peaceful-revolution era of the 1990s in the united Germany and its Eastern neighbours.

Turning to Western Europe, there can be little doubt that 1992 will mark a watershed in European banking. The ability of any bank to operate in every EEC member country on the basis of a single licence will increase competition as the 'newcomers' seek out the most lucrative segments of the financial markets, leaving the 'locals' to deal with the dross.

A survey by the Bank of England in 1989 on the views of British banks and financial institutions of the effects of the Single European Market revealed:

(a) Change will be evolutionary rather than sudden.
(b) There will be more opportunities than threats.
(c) Major corporate products and services will be the first to create a single market, due in part to their wholesaling being already international.
(d) Retail markets will remain fragmented for some time due to national characteristics.
(e) Competition from the United States and Japan is likely to have more impact on the British market than will competition from within the EEC.

We shall now consider how these two major competitors are shaping up for the 1990s and their likely effects on ethical banking.

2.3   TRENDS IN AMERICAN BANKING

Just as the universal bank will provide a model in Europe, the 1990 banking model in the United States will be the 'super-regional bank'. At the start of the 1980s such a bank did not exist; by 1990 there were over twenty with combined assets of more than £600 billion. Super-regional banks operate in more than one state. They are a consequence of a Supreme Court ruling to change the situation which had existed in the United States since the Pepper–McFadden Act.

Seeking to prevent a concentration of financial power, that Act prevented banks in one state from operating full branches in another. An unforeseen consequence of the Act, however, was the growth of the so-called money banks such as Citicorp, Bankers Trust, Chase in New York.

The new super-regionals now want a larger slice of the national banking market which the 'New York giants' formerly shared among themselves.

In recent years, some super-regionals have suffered large losses from bad property loans, but their woes were less than those of the money banks with their enormous exposure to Third World loans.

The super-regionals are now sorting themselves into the three categories of

— highly successful,
— successful,
— unsuccessful.

The highly successful are those like North Carolina's NCNB Corporation which have a clear vision and which concentrate on what they do best. (In this respect they are no different from any other highly successful company.) What most seem to do best is lend to medium-size companies. Cost control is a critical factor in these far-flung banks located in a number of states. Wells Fargo is the outstanding cost-controller. The successful super-regionals are those which have merged with or acquired compatible partners and have maintained steady rather than speedy growth, such as Fleet/Norster which runs two regional banks and several other businesses.

The unsuccessful are those which have become embroiled in post-merger drift or have concentrated their lending in a falling property market such as the Bank of New England.

As legislation changes the super-regionals will grow by acquisition and will become real competitors of the money banks. Citicorp is the only one of these which seems ready to battle with the super-regional. Its main weapon is technology. It has used its electronic networks and data banks to build itself into a national bank.

One outcome of these trends in the United States is that super-regionals will become owned by 'non-banks', major manufacturing companies which have no banking traditions and different ethical codes – for better or worse – than the banking industry. Another outcome will be ownership by foreign banks and other institutions. We have already seen in this chapter that some leading super-regionals in California are owned by the Japanese; this is a trend which will grow and will influence ethical banking in the United States.

2.4 TRENDS IN JAPANESE BANKING

Adapting the British description of US Forces during the war: 'Over-paid, oversexed and over here', the Japanese banking industry can be described as 'overregulated, overcrowded and over everywhere'. Nine of the ten top banks world-wide are Japanese; the world's largest securities house, Nomura, is Japanese.

In recent years, the Japanese have paid heavily for their aggressive overseas expansion resulting in painful write-offs of Mexican debt. The Japanese banks are highly regulated at home; this makes the freer conditions of other financial markets highly attractive. Although there is no immediate prospect of dismantling the legal barriers which separate different types of Japanese banks and securities companies, the very prospect of change is unsettling the industry.

Medium and small companies have become the key sectors for lending as the Japanese multimarket has grown financially self-sufficient. Sources of cheap money which fuelled the growth of Japanese banks have dried up as government restrictions on interest rates are removed. The competition for funds from rich industrialists has grown rapidly causing the banks to respond to greater competition from life assurance and securities companies.

For many years Japanese banks have held huge portfolios of securities of client companies. These have been 'loss leaders', the cost of the low-yielding stock from the client and the growth in market value of the shares. Now that large companies are no longer borrowing and the stock-market is becoming more turbulent there will be a temptation to sell off the shares.

The financial markets in Japan are likely to become more volatile in the 1990s as the regulatory frameworks are taken down and replaced by new rules. The United States and the European Community are unlikely to tolerate the growth of Japanese influence in their markets without enjoying reciprocal rights.

As the Japanese respond to these pressures their influence on new ethical banking will grow. The Judaeo-Christian and Hellenic philosophies, with their emphases on free will and truth and individual accountability, will have to adjust to that of Shintoism with its emphasis on collective duty and loyalty to superiors. While it would be wrong to suggest that one tradition is ethically superior to the other, it is important to recognise that they lead to different types of ethical behaviour. So too does another philosophy which is now a major world force and will influence the new ethical banking – Islam.

2.5   TRENDS IN ISLAMIC BANKING

Islamic banking is a relatively new phenomenon. It was only in 1950 that Saudi Arabia established its own currency; Islamic banking (as distinct from European banks in the Middle East) began to develop in the 1960s. The oil boom of the 1970s spurred the growth of Islamic banks, but the main impetus in the spread of Islamic values in banking came with the revolution in Iran. Today, only that country and Pakistan have adopted the system completely but its influence spreads across the globe. In Britain, estimates of the volume of business conducted by banks conforming to Islamic principles range from $1 to $5 billion; world-wide the estimates are from $20 to $40 billion and growing.

There are three categories of Islamic banks in operation:

(1) Islamic development banks which concentrate on economic development in the Third World.
(2) Islamic commercial banks which are similar in the scope of their operations to British and American commercial banks.
(3) Commercial banks which offer a limited range of Islamic products.

What links these categories together is the Koran; they all operate in varying degrees in accordance with the principles of *Sharia* or Islamic law.

The objectives of Islamic banking are:

— to attract funds and employ these resources in Islamic countries;
— to develop the saving habit among Muslim individuals;
— to offer interest-free bank services according to Islamic Shariah.

The seven financial instruments of Islamic banking are:

(a) Mudaraba – unit trust agreement
(b) Murabaha – resale contract
(c) Musharaka – a venture partnership
(d) Ijara – leasing
(e) Wadia – pawnbroking-type agreement
(f) Takafol – mutual insurance
(g) Qard Hasan – loan without interest

These practices are described more fully in Table 2.1. Most Islamic banking practices are cumbersome and can be in conflict with Western banking legislation. They depend on very high levels of trust.

The Islamic prohibition on charging any interest on loans can have unusual consequences. An example is quoted by Hashi Syedain in a survey of Islamic banking in *Management Today*, May 1989. Many Moslems in Britain have used the services of an Islamic bank to finance house purchase. Interest-free house purchase is arranged by a combination of *musharaka* (venture principle) and *ijara* (leasing). Benefit is taken of British trust laws which make a distinction between legal and beneficial ownership. 'The bank and its customer buy a property together and the customer then buys back the bank's share by instalments at cost price. The bank makes its profit by leasing its interest in the house to the customer at a rate fixed on a yearly basis . . . There is one significant catch – because there is no interest involved, customers do not qualify for mortgage tax relief.'

As far as ethical banking is concerned, Islamic banking is important because it raises a number of alternative approaches to the banker–customer relationship. It helps to stimulate new thinking about alternative banking and possible ethical solutions to emerging problems, such as coping with the underclass and financing small businesses based on networks or communes. Regardless of our views on the merits or otherwise of Islam, what we are witnessing is the growth of a type of banking which states its ethical values explicitly.

Table 2.1　Islamic banking practices

MUDARABA – a unit trust-type agreement between a bank (the lender) and a businessman whereby the bank agrees to finance a project on a profit or loss sharing basis. The businessman undertakes to pay back the capital invested and a share of the profits. He acts as project manager while the bank acts as capital provider.

MURABAHA – a resale contract whereby the client requests the bank to buy specific goods. The bank resells these at a price which covers the purchase price plus the profit margin agreed upon by both parties. This changes traditional lending into a sale and purchase agreement, under which the bank buys the goods wanted by the client for resale to the client at a higher price agreed upon by both parties.

MUSHARAKA – a partnership for a specific business activity, in which the bank and the partner create joint venture projects with the aim of making a profit, whereby, like the German universal bank concept, there is a participation in the management.

IJARA – straightforward leasing, renting or hiring.

WADIA – an agreement to deposit an asset (excluding land) into the custody of the bank.

TAKAFOL – mutual support whereby the various participants agree to pay instalments into a fund managed by the bank. The bank acts as a management company – admitting participants, collecting instalments, investing funds and paying benefits – under the conditions of the contract.

QARD HASAN – literally a 'good loan'. This is a loan whereby a borrower is obliged to repay the lender the principal sum borrowed on the loan. It is left to the discretion of the borrower to reward the lender for his loan by paying any sum over and above the amount of the principal. Usually this is used in a transaction between the state and a less wealthy member of society.

2.6　ETHICS AND CULTURE

The significance for ethical banking of this growth in internationalism of banks is plain to see. It has long been recognised that there are wide differences in what is ethically acceptable, both across national cultures and over time within a single culture. Lying is, in most Western cultures, considered more wrong than in Eastern cultures where the 'wrongness' depends on the context in which the lie occurs.

The Japanese place a higher value on social harmony as an ethical goal than they do on truthfulness. In Japan, a person has a moral duty to lie in certain social situations.

The core elements of ethical behaviour are determined by time and circumstances shaping society. A country under constant military threat will emphasise physical courage and have no moral qualms about treating its perceived enemies in ways which others consider to be unethical. One has only to look at Israel, Cambodia and El Salvador for examples of this phenomenon.

An affluent society will emphasise charity towards needy persons. Britain in the 1980s was an example of such a society where charities emerged in great numbers to stir the conscience of rich individuals. The drive by some banks and building societies to provide charity-oriented credit cards, whereby a tiny proportion of a customer's credit turnover is allocated to a designated charity, can be seen either as a spur to social conscience or a cynical exploitation of a trend.

In contrast to rich society, poor societies, such as India, develop a moral code which encourages detachment from the poor and the sick. Hence the work of Mother Teresa which we hold up as an example of virtue in the West is perceived, in a sense, as 'unethical' in the Indian subcontinent. The growing number of poor across the world is another force shaping ethical banking.

2.7 TRENDS IN ALTERNATIVE BANKING

There are four types of alternative banks (and alternatives to banks) which are influencing ethical banking since they are based on more explicit ethical values than are the traditional banks:

— Social collateral banking
— Viewpoint banking
— Mutual societies
— 'Ethical' investments

2.7.1 Social Collateral Banking

This began in Bangladesh in 1977. The problem of poor people without ownership of homes or land is acute in that country. Such people find it impossible to raise loans and invest in improving their standard of living. The Grameen Bank has addressed this problem by developing a system of social 'collateral'. People wanting to use the bank are asked to organise themselves into groups of fifty and subgroups of five. Members of each subgroup are asked to act as guarantor for each other's loans. Each group and subgroup also act as the evaluator and approver of each loan. Thus 'credit scoring' moves from the bank to the community.

The success of this non-traditional approach can be gauged by the traditional measures of banking: a 97.3 per cent on-time repayment of loans totalling over £54 million to more than 290 000 borrowers, three-quarters of whom are women. And the bank makes a profit.

Social collateral banking is moving into India and South America. It is also catching on in the affluent West – South Shore Bank of Chicago and Mercury Provident in the UK are experimenting with ways of using social collateral to lend to the so-called underclass.

2.7.2 Viewpoint Banking

This is my term for alternative banks based on a shared philosophy or viewpoint (Islamic banking is the prime example). Mercury Provident, mentioned in the previous paragraph, is a British 'licensed deposit taker' whose clients tend to share the ideas of Rudolph Steiner. An 'ecologist' ahead of this time, Steiner viewed money as a representation of social and spiritual energy. It should be used in a fully conscious way – knowing where it is going and the purposes for which it is being used.

Members of Mercury Provident can have an account similar to a building society savings account – but with some differences. They can specify their own terms of withdrawal and their own rates of interest (up to a specified ceiling). Each member can specify either a particular project or area of work to which they want their money to be lent. By this means both lenders and borrowers become much more aware of each other's interests. Projects financed by Mercury Provident range from publishing to retirement homes, as well as investments in organics research, Steiner schools and Marged Shoes (a women's cooperative making shoes in Wales). Mercury Provident uses National Westminster as its clearing bank.

Another example of viewpoint banking is doing without conventional currency. Pioneered in Canada under the title Local Employment and Trade System (LETS System) it has spread to the US, Australia, New Zealand and Britain.

The system is designed not to replace conventional currency completely, but as a complementary system that helps local communities to thrive independently of national and international economics. LETS uses a 'Green pound' to replace barter trading; Green pounds are intangible, existing only in the books and computers of the system and are created simply by trading. It works as follows. Whenever someone trades with another member, for example buying food or renting a room, they simply inform the 'office' which debits one account and credits the other. The buyer need not have any Green pounds to start buying, and there is no interest charged anywhere in the system. The creation of 'money' is linked solely to the creation of real value, so no one can hoard money and profit from other people's shortage.

LETS is still in the experimental stage but it has lessons for the new ethical banking. It requires active participation rather than passive consumption. More importantly, it focuses on the need for trust, commitment from members and skilful management.

2.7.3 Mutual Societies

Mutual societies are not new; they are the concept behind the building society movement. However, as building societies move to become banks there is another long-established form of mutuality which is gaining strength – credit unions.

In the US, there are now 14 000 credit unions, in Nigeria 7000; total assets are over $200 billion. Thus the credit union movement is significantly larger than Islamic banking. In Britain, there are around 150 credit unions and some local authorities are supporting their growth. There are credit unions among London taxi drivers, the Pentecostal Church and many local communities.

A credit union is a mutual financial cooperative which offers savings and low-interest loans to its members. Members save a regular amount each week and borrow from the common pool as and when they need to. By law a credit union must be formed by people sharing a 'common bond'. This can mean working for the same employer or resident in the same area, or members of the same association.

In Britain, the Credit Union Act of 1979 provides the legal framework within which credit unions must operate. Currently, the maximum interest rate is 1 per cent a month for borrowers and a maximum of 8 per cent for savers. Loans and savings are limited to a maximum of £2000.

2.7.4 'Ethical' Investments

These are not a new phenomenon but are the fastest growing 'new idea' in banking.

Since the mid 1980s an increasing number of conventional banks has offered 'ethical investment funds'. By this they mean companies which are engaged in producing environmentally friendly products as distinct from companies involved in armaments, animal testing for products, harmful chemicals, or South Africa.

Lines can become blurred in these categories. To assist investors in making the 'right' choice, the Ethical Investment Research and Information Service (EIRIS) was started in 1983. It provides lists of acceptable companies given particular criteria. It emphasises that it does not 'make judgements about the moral acceptability of the activities of individual firms', but it can tell potential investors a company's policy on arms, nuclear power or South Africa.

We have already seen that Mercury Provident predated the new enlightenment of so-called ethical investment funds. Another 'pioneer' is the Ecology Building Society.

Founded in 1981 with only ten members and £5000, it now has assets of over £4 million. The Ecology Building Society operates similarly to its long-established counterparts, lending its money as mortgages on property. Where it differs from other societies is in its criteria for lending which shall be 'most likely to lead to the saving of non-renewable resources, the promotion of self-sufficiency in individuals or communities, or the most ecologically efficient use of land'. This must surely be one of the most value-laden criteria of any financial institution. For ethical banking it holds a lesson – beware of being over zealous in imposing your values on customers. For example, the Ecology Building Society will lend to an organically farmed smallholding, but not to barn conversions for holiday homes, no matter how much they improve the local environment.

All the examples of alternative banking described in this section are a reality. Each signals a trend which conventional banks need to take into account:

(a) extending the criteria for lending;
(b) giving more decision-making to customers on where their money is invested;
(c) devising new ways of meeting the financial needs of the poor.

At the other end of the spectrum from helping the poor is helping the rich to safeguard and increase their wealth. This is no new challenge for banks but it is one which is receiving increased attention in the new ethical banking.

2.8 BANKS FOR THE RICH

For bankers, the rich, like the poor, are always with us. But they like to be treated differently.

Mass market banks are a relatively recent phenomenon. For legal reasons, they have not existed in the United States. In Britain, they are less than a hundred years old, being a response to the growth of industry at the turn of the century, but only coming into active life as purveyors of a range of saving and lending products on a vast scale since the 1960s.

The 1980s in both Britain and the United States have seen an unprecedented growth in affluence. The common millionaire has given way to the billionaire. Senior executives receive six-figure salaries; entrepreneurs have become 'seriously rich' in their thirties, dealers in the money markets have become seriously rich and seriously poor in their twenties.

In 1987, the most wealthy 10 per cent of the adult population of the UK owned half the total marketable wealth. This minority has been passionately courted by the banks; the day of the personal banker has arrived. Personal knowledge of clients' individual circumstances and the ability to respond to them swiftly and flexibly is the main selling point of small banks.

One characteristic is to appear to eschew modern technology by providing detailed account statements. Drummonds (a subsidiary of the Royal Bank of Scotland), located at Charing Cross in London, panders to this nostalgia by providing customers with quill pens and even snuff on request.

The management of assets tends to be dealt with in an impersonal manner by the large clearing banks. Not so in the old and new private banks. Duncan Lawrie, founded in London in 1971, manages funds of its clients of at least £45 000 at a 1 per cent charge plus VAT. Unlike Duncan Lawrie, most private banks on both sides of the Atlantic are subsidiaries of large banks. In Britain, the largest and best known 'private bank', Coutts, with fourteen branches, is owned by the National Westminster Bank. The Royal Bank of Scotland has three private banks under its wing: (i) Child and Co. which caters particularly for the law and bloodstock industries; (ii) Holts which focuses on the armed services; (iii) Drummonds which caters particularly for affluent Scots who have exiled themselves to London.

In the US, the parentage of private banks is more clearly identified. One of the largest – American Express Bank – advertises the traits which it seeks in its 'élite corps' of bankers:

Character. Cast iron integrity, energy, stamina, and grace under pressure.
Verve. We admire activists who are willing to break some china within the bank in order to be effective for their clients.
Entrepreneurship. We reward those whose solutions to one client's needs create fertile opportunities for other clients.
Unselfishness. Every Account Officer must be a 'switchboard' connecting clients with *whoever* will best serve their needs.
Resilience. People who thrive on weeks of sustained effort, and who display a genius for keeping up with change.

Putting to one side copy-writers' hyperbole, this mixture of ethical values and physical characteristics does at least attempt to reveal an ethical code, particularly the definition of 'unselfishness'. This is one of the contributions which both private banks and the more specialised 'banking boutiques' can make to ethical values – a spelling out of what they stand for.

In America, private banking concentrates on lending to affluent individuals; in Switzerland, the primary focus is on investment management with particular emphasis on the preservation of capital and assurance of secrecy, though this is now under threat.

The private banker provides a highly personalised service and charges for it accordingly. They are masters of the relationship approach to banking rather than the more common transactional approach. This is difficult for the larger banks to provide, hence there will be an increasing trend by the major banks in Britain and elsewhere to set up private bank subsidiaries, probably under a different name. The Coutts–National Westminster relationship and the three offshoots of the Royal Bank of Scotland provide a model.

One other contribution which the private bank phenomenon will make to ethical banking is a greater openness by all banks on their charges and on criteria for opening an account. The rich are generally more demanding than the poor; they like to know what they will be charged for their banking services. Therefore, as more 'private banks' are estalished by the large banks (and building societies which have transformed into banks), there will be pressure from consumers' groups, and probably legislation, to force banks to be more open about charges to all their customers. The key issue will be not so much the amount charged but the ability of a bank, or rather a branch manager, to *justify* the level of charge to the satisfaction of customers.

Another contribution to ethical banking will be to force larger banks to devise a type of customer interaction which blends the relationship approach with the transactional approach. This I call the 'situational approach'.

2.9 THE SITUATIONAL APPROACH

As major banks have grown it has proved increasingly difficult to provide the relationship approach of serving the needs of each customer through an in-depth knowledge of the individual and his/her personal circumstances built up over many years. This has not solely been the fault of banks. Customers have become more geographically mobile; also, the spread of services through ATMs has kept the customer out of contact. Indeed, the manager has become increasingly like the priest in the confessional, meeting only those who have sinned.

The transactional approach with its focus on relating to customers on a series of one-off contacts based on a specific transaction be it a home loan or insurance purchase, has become more common. This is probably due to the numbers of customers who have to be serviced and also to the proliferation of products, each accompanied by a sales drive.

A further factor is the use of credit scoring which leads to each loan application being treated separately. This can also apply in loan applications being evaluated by a lending officer.

The situational approach would require that every customer with a certain amount of assets deposited with the bank should be contacted annually and offered the opportunity to discuss their financial situation and ways in which the bank might help them. This would include determining if they are getting the best deal on their investments, taking account of their needs and priorities. For example, by being pro-active in offering to transfer funds to a higher interest account, a branch manager might find that the customer has preference for accessibility which makes the existing arrangements more satisfactory. Equally, every customer with credit facilities over a certain sum should have an annual meeting with an appropriate bank official to review the situation and determine whether there are alternative arrangements to his/her benefit.

Situational banking is not altruism. The risk of losing a few interest points has to be set against the risk of the customer closing the account and transferring the business to a competitor.

2.10   TRENDS IN TECHNOLOGY

Few industries have undergone the technology revolution of banking. Billions of pounds have been invested in the establishment of networks, the development of ATMs/cash machines, the provision of on-line data to branches and even to clients. Looking ahead, the two major technological innovations in banking will be the use of the telephone and the television.

Telephone banking enables customers to phone and interrogate their banks' computer system and be answered by a recorded voice. Midland Bank has gone further and provides the customers of their First Direct telephone banking service with a response from a human operator. Their prelaunch research showed that the vast majority of people prefer to talk to people rather than computers. At the time of writing, it is too early to assess the success or otherwise of First Direct.

However, the longer established computer response systems have got off to a slow start in Britain. Only twenty of over 600 banks and building societies provide this type of service. Just over 1 million customers use the system, the TSB group accounting for a quarter of the total.

There are three types of telephone banking systems in operation:

(1) Modern telephone
(2) Tone pads
(3) Voice recognition

The modern telephone with its push buttons for dialling enables the customer to give the account and personal identification number. The customer then dials different numbers for different services – updated account statement, new cheque book, etc. Customers can also pay bills and use other bank services by telephone, provided they have completed the necessary documentation at their branch to set up the system.

Tone pads – small electronic units which imitate the bleeps made by a telephone – are provided by some banks to customers who do not have the modern phones. The procedure for using the telephone banking service using the tone pad is the same as with the modern telephone.

Voice recognition is still in its infancy, being pioneered by the Royal Bank of Scotland. There are three types of voice response systems:

(a) 'Voice print'. This is the most sophisticated system. The words of the customer are compared to a voice print which is stored in the customer's branch. Only when the two match can any transaction take place. The number of words which can be recognised is limited.

(b) 'Isolated words'. This system recognises a spoken digit at a time and simple words like 'yes', 'no', between a 'bleep'.

(c) 'Continuing digits'. This allows a complete string of numbers to be uttered for recognition to take place.

Telephone technology, like the use of ATMs, raises problems of confidentiality. Furthermore, a voice recognition system which mistakes one digit for another can cause problems for both bank and customer.

Ethical banking will require a drawing up of codes of conduct for banking technology.

Television banking has been pioneered by the Bank of Scotland under the acronym HOBS (Home and Office Banking Service). This allows customers to check details of their accounts and order services over the telephone line by pressing a key pad in front of their television set. A simple, cheap keyboard (£100) plugs into the television and the telephone. When used, the television will show on its screen the information sought by the customer. Providing prior arrangements have been made, HOBS will pay bills 'just in time' to gain maximum credit. It also makes easier the transfer of funds from one account to another to gain maximum interest. The technological effectiveness of HOBS is restricted by the inadequacies of customers' televisions. The provision of data on screens is sometimes blurred and it can take, in computer terms, a long time to respond to instructions.

More sophisticated types of television banking, using personal computers, are on the horizon. The spread of this type of banking will increase. It is feasible for a Japanese bank to service the needs of British customers from Tokyo without having to open a single branch. Though that time may be far off, it is necessary now to establish codes of conduct which will be in accord with the canons of ethical banking described in the next chapter.

2.11 CONCLUSION

The future shape of banking will result from the monumental changes taking place in the industry across the world. Increasing customer sophistication will force banks to design and deliver products in new ways to take advantage of the growing internationalism of banking.

In Europe, the Second Banking Directive which allows banks to establish themselves in other countries will lead to new alliances and increased competition for lucrative niches. The concept of the universal bank pioneered in Germany will spread its wings in the new Germany and in Eastern Europe.

Super-regional banks, increasingly owned by 'non-banks' will capture much of the US domestic market, forcing the giant money banks to be more aggressive overseas. Changes in the legal framework of Japanese banking will have consequences which will reverberate across the globe as the Japanese giants flex their muscles. New forms of banking drawing on different value systems will appear and be treated as either a threat or a source of inspiration by traditional banks. The need to provide a personal touch for more demanding and increasingly affluent customers will spur the development of 'private banking'. Large banks will need to offer different levels of service, and for their core of customers will adopt a 'situational approach'. In addition, the march of technology will continue with greater use of telephones and television to enable customers to be served at home.

All these trends will raise new ethical issues and revive some old ones. There will be a need to think through the principles on which banks will respond to new needs from their customers and new pressures from their competitors. Banking will be a more demanding and exciting industry to work in; the question is, faced with all these changes will it be more or less ethical?

3 Ethics – the Engine of Behaviour

3.1 INTRODUCTION

Ethics are the engine of our behaviour, they drive us towards some behaviour and away from others. We acquire our ethics from various sources; parents, teachers, leaders, colleagues, employers, religion, all contribute.

As children we acquire from our parents an orientation towards ethics – what is 'good' or 'bad' – which we may rebel against as we grow older. Children think in specific terms rather than in abstracts. They tend to be ethical because it pleases someone they admire. They do not think in terms of ethical standards.

When we grow older we begin to make decisions for ourselves. Young adulthood is the most formative stage in our ethical development. In our twenties we are faced with decisions on career, marriage, location and their effects on relatives and parenthood. These decisions force us to test our ethics. Whether we want to be ethical in a particular situation depends on a variety of factors:

— our ability to identify the ethical issues;
— our proficiency at problem solving;
— our capacity to anticipate and weigh risks;
— our competence in implementing the decision with minimal hurt to ourselves and others.

These factors continue to come into play as we grow older and are confronted with problems of business ethics in our work. This book is not about 'teaching' ethics but is concerned with providing guidelines and examples against which you can measure your ethical behaviour. My intention is to heighten awareness of the forces which are impacting on banking as a whole and to help the individual 'banker' (regardless of job title) to respond to these forces in an ethical manner. The focus is on ethical decision-making, which means challenging many of the traditional and current assumptions made by bankers.

29

3.2   ASSUMPTIONS ABOUT ETHICS

Ethics are not synonymous with law or religion. Law defines standards of behaviour which must be complied with under threat of
specified penalties for violation. Some laws do coincide with ethical
behaviour – it is unlawful and unethical to murder an individual.
(Killing a person in self-defence is not unethical though the circumstances may make it unlawful.) Parking in a 'no parking zone' is
unlawful but not unethical; though parking without need in a disabled parking bay is both unlawful and unethical.

The banking industry has witnessed a cascade of new laws in recent
years, many of which are intended to reinforce ethical standards. But
as we shall see later, the impact of the laws can lead to the growth of
unethical behaviour. Talking of the United States (but it could apply
also to Britain), William Schreyer, Chairman of the financial giant
Merrill Lynch, said, 'With our national litigation binge, we've seen a
shift from a moral standard to a legal standard. It becomes not what
you should do, but what your lawyers can find a loophole for.'

Ethics are not laws; they are not adopted by some legislative body
with the power to enforce them. However, in some professions (not
banking) ethics have, in effect, the force of law. 'Unethical behaviour', as defined in their profession, can lead to doctors, dentists and
lawyers being 'struck off' and hence deprived of practising their
vocation. Bankers may suffer opprobrium from their fellows if found
guilty of misconduct, they may even go to jail, but it is still possible
for them to return to making a living in banking and financial
services.

Ethics are not religion; a value system based on beliefs in some
form of the supernatural which can result in certain behaviour which
may or may not be legal or ethical. For example, a religious group
may be declared unlawful, but its adherents will believe they have a
moral duty to continue to practise it. Some religions may require
behaviour which the majority of society considers unethical; for
example, refusing to give a dying child proper medical attention.

An individual can practise his/her religion secretly whereas ethics
are normally practised in the public domain. Ethics are usage and
custom among members of a specific group which are reflected in the
behaviour of both the individual and the group to one another and to
the public they serve. The core of ethical behaviour lies in the
question: how would I want to be treated if I was in that situation?

There is both a practical and a spiritual dimension to ethics. The practical dimension shows itself in our caring for fellow beings, the spiritual dimension in our sense of right and wrong.

3.3   ETHICAL DECISION-MAKING

Ethical issues arise in times of uncertainty and in situations of ambiguity. If it is clear to all concerned that there is a 'right' decision to be made, there is, in effect, no decision to be made by an individual; the law of the situation determines the decision. But often in banking we are faced with decisions in shades of grey rather than black or white. This is where ethical decision-making has to take place.

Faced with a major problem, it is desirable to consider three different solutions; one of them is virtually certain to be ethical. There are two levels in ethical decision-making:

— First, separate the clearly unethical decisions from the ethical ones. Lying, stealing, injuring others are obviously unethical.
— Second, you may need to choose between ethical values.

The second point is a key issue for the new ethical banker. For example, a choice may have to be made between truth and loyalty or truth and fairness where no one answer is absolutely right or absolutely wrong. The individual has to analyse the situation as clearly as possible and be sensitive to what are the most important values. Care has to be taken to avoid trading-off an ethical value and an unethical one. For instance, it is acceptable to sacrifice truth for fairness, but not to sacrifice truth for greater profit.

In new ethical banking, one ethical principle can only be sacrificed for another. The importance of this will become apparent when we consider the canons of ethical banking. There is undoubtedly some sacrifice involved in being ethical, but this is far outweighed by its positive effect on personal, corporate and social well-being in the long term.

To sum up on ethics in general terms, there are two levels of behaviour to be considered. On one level is the law, an increasing factor in all banking and financial activities. But no law has yet been written that the ingenious cannot circumvent. So at a higher level there is a need to encourage people to recognise and accept that underlying any law is a social ideal that seeks to improve society.

The new ethical banker should do more than he is required to do and less than he is allowed to do. He needs to exercise judgement, self-restraint and conscience. This is nothing new for the vast majority of bankers; what is new and ever changing is the context in which ethical behaviour has to be exercised. That is the issue which binds together the subsequent chapters of this book.

3.4 DEVELOPING ETHICAL AWARENESS

LaRue Hosmer, who has the unusual title of Professor of Corporate Strategy and Managerial Ethics at the University of Michigan, in the US, observes: 'Maybe you can't teach moral standards, but you can teach people how to analyse questions so as to bring to bear whatever moral standards they have' (*Enterprise Magazine*, April 1989).

Any such ethical education should address three questions:

(1) How do you identify an ethical problem?
(2) How do you deal with it?
(e) How can a manager get his subordinates to act ethically?

Some ethical problems stand out for all to see. These are usually the types of problem which anyone with an ounce of moral sense will avoid. More difficult are those which sneak up and catch individuals unawares. These are most likely to occur when an industry is undergoing change, as is banking and financial services. The 'greedy 80s' have thrown up many examples of individuals using the prevailing uncertainty surrounding banking to push to the limit of sound ethics and beyond. Ivan Boesky, Michael Milken and their opposite numbers in the City of London are obvious examples.

Another source of unforeseen ethical problems can occur when there are intensive economic and competitive pressures. There is a temptation to cut corners, to pass off unethical decisions as matters of economic necessity, such as redundancy. People who have given a lifetime of dedicated service suddenly find themselves unemployed, unemployable and struggling on a minimal pension. (See 'The Loyal Employees Problem' on page 207.)

Ethical behaviour begins with the recognition that the choices you make have consequences for others. In making your choices and anticipating the consequences, there are a number of tools which can help:

(a) Golden rules against which you measure your proposed behaviour – do unto others as you would have them do unto you.
(b) Mirror-testing – how would I feel about explaining my behaviour to my children?
(c) Codes of conduct.

More elaborate devices are covered in Chapter 8, 'Developing Ethical Bankers'. For the present, we shall review trends in business ethics on both sides of the Atlantic.

3.5 TRENDS IN BUSINESS ETHICS

In the first *Banker* Lecture given at the IMF World Bank meeting in 1988, Chips Keswick, Chairman of Hambros, argued that the main hope for banking in the 1990s is a return to the old virtues of common sense and integrity and an avoidance of the seesaws of fashion. Keswick felt that bankers must be allowed to exercise their own judgement on what their money is doing rather than become increasingly subject to the dictates of a growing bureaucracy of regulators.

Dealing with the limits of legislation, Keswick said:

> The monumental error of judgement is the belief in some quarters that you can codify integrity. The Ancient Greeks failed to, as did the Romans; and the chicanery since the Industrial Revolution has continued the impossibility. There is nothing sillier than a person drafting a law for integrity. My own observation suggests that 95% of those who work in banks are honest people; most of the remaining 5% can be kept straight by a mixture of strong leadership and fear of being caught. There will always be a tiny minority of genuinely dishonest people. These will only be frustrated by sound internal systems and the vigilance of management. Integrity must come from within; it can never be successfully imposed from without. (*The Banker*, October 1988)

He went on to imply the need for defining ethical banking standards by saying:

Customers are, of course, entitled to reliably high standards [of ethics] and the assurance that those who handle their money are maintaining those standards. But this cannot, in my view, be achieved by weighty legislation and reliance upon juries and the inadequacies of criminal law. This contention is well supported by the very low conviction success for fraud cases in the UK criminal courts. It can best be achieved by the jealous stewardship of professional standards by those within the financial world, with the wide powers of striking off or removal of licence practised by many other professional bodies. (ibid)

What lessons on business ethics can bankers learn from the experience of other professional bodies and other countries?

Business ethics are a major preoccupation of management in the United States. It has been on the curriculum of Harvard Business School since 1915, being expanded after the crash of 1929. Today, the ethical consequences of management decisions run as a thread through all Harvard courses. Over 90 per cent of America's 2000 largest companies have ethical codes of practice for all employees; many companies run ethics education programmes. An *Economist* report (7 July 1989) summarised a number of issues arising from trends in the United States:

— Cynics argue that ethics will be forgotten when business conditions worsen. Not so, said John Ackers, Chairman of IBM, 'Ethics and competitiveness are inseparable . . . the greater the measure of mutual trust and confidence in the ethics of a society, the greater its economic strength.'
— Ethical codes are increasingly being applied in global, and not just national, terms. For example, Levi-Strauss, a jeans manufacturer, forbids bribes 'whether or not prevalent or legal in the foreign country involved'.
— A growing number of companies have board level ethics committees responsible for ethics policy, arranging ethics seminars for employees, ordering regular ethics audits. (These approaches are developed in Chapter 8.)
— A small but increasing number of companies have set up independent ethics offices or ombudsmen as a channel for employees who feel that they have been penalised for raising matters which they considered unethical on the part of their manager.

A more questionable practice is for a company to take an ethical initiative and then press for it to become law. *The Economist* (7 July 1989) reports the case of Cummins Engine, a diesel-engine manufacturer, which cleaned up its engines and then lobbied for tougher pollution laws.

Looking at the situation of business ethics in Britain at the end of the 1980s, Pamela Pocock, a director of consultants Strategic People, told personnel managers at their annual conference in 1989: 'The ethics of any business are simply a reflection of the values demonstrated in that business and, if we are to examine values, we must necessarily consider the issue of culture, since values are the bedrock of corporate culture . . . At a fundamental level we must assume that organisation's wish to behave ethically.' Pocock went on to describe five factors which interfered with this assumed aspiration:

(1) Moral relativism – ethics are adjusted to suit the circumstances.
(2) Acceptance of ethical erosion – individuals and groups conspire to cover up some unethical act.
(3) The corporate mean of mediocrity – conformance leading to complacency and intolerance of the 'maverick' or 'whistle blower'.
(4) Short-termism – acceptance of inconsistency in ethical behaviour because each case is viewed individually and in terms of short-term consequences.
(5) Separation of corporate and private morality – acceptance of a separation in personal and public ethical behaviour.

We can apply these five ethical time-bombs to banking.

3.6 ETHICAL TIME-BOMBS

Moral relativism shows itself in banking when rules are bent to suit a particular customer. This does not mean that every customer must be treated alike in terms of service, but that regardless of the business consequences ethical standards must be complied with.

Management has a key role to play here in educating both staff and customers. By being seen to comply with defined ethical standards you will benefit from staff following your ethical leadership and from customers knowing that they will all be treated fairly.

Acceptance of moral erosion has shown itself in such events as:

— The non-disclosure of their holding of Blue Arrow shares by County Natwest and the Union Bank of Switzerland to hide the relative failure of the Blue Arrow launch.
— The cover-up of illegal share dealings in the Guinness/Distillers affair.
— The fabrication of the background of the Al Fayed brothers in their bid for Harrods.

In every case there were 'victims': careers were destroyed, individuals suffered, more ethically concerned businesses were tarnished with the phrase, 'They're all the same'.

It is a salutary fact that in the aftermath of the Drexel Burnham Lambert failure on Wall Street (which reverberated through the international banking world) a poll of 404 senior executives in the United States by *Business Week* (March 1990) revealed an insight into the acceptance of moral erosion. Over 70 per cent felt that Drexel's actions were bad for the United States and were not sorry to see them go. Of the 35 per cent who had used Drexel, a stunning 74 per cent said that *the firm's ethics were no different from those of its competitors*.

A frightening example of the complete erosion of ethical standards was revealed in the trial in 1990 of four City brokers. Typical comments on the unfortunate clients were:

— 'Go easy. Make him some money, then get the bastard for 100k. He is very smart.'
— 'Nice chap, could be a big big loser.'
— Of a retired headmaster who invested £1500, '. . . soft old man. I don't think he will survive any serious churning.'
— 'Anyone stupid enough to send money on the strength of a telephone call deserves to lose it.'
— 'Never mind whether they win or lose, just keep the money coming in.'

Admittedly, this was an extreme case which was dealt with by the courts. But are there not situations in 'respectable' banks when faint echoes of these cynical sentiments may be heard?

The ethical time-bomb labelled 'the corporate mean of mediocrity' is particularly relevant to banks. Most employees have not known, and will not know, any other employment. Because of generous pension, loan and mortgage arrangements they have more at stake in their company than do most employees in other industries. There is, therefore, strong pressure to conform to the prevailing culture and to be intolerant of mavericks. Furthermore, misconceived confidentiality can dissuade an employee from reporting perceived unethical behaviour. On the other hand, banks do have strong audit or inspection functions and finance houses have 'conformance officials'; there are also many regulatory bodies at work. All these tend to deal with major breaches of the law. It is in the day to day situations in a small town branch that the pressures to conform can cause temporary blindness to questionable ethical practices.

The fourth ethical time-bomb, short-termism, is a consequence of judging individual and company results on a monthly or quarterly basis. Special sales drives to push a particular product, almost regardless of its appropriateness to the customers, is another explosive ingredient. The hope of being able to retrieve a situation before being 'found out' is not peculiar to banking. However, it can lead the way to fraud, unhealthy banker–customer collusion and a general lowering of ethical standards.

The last ethical time-bomb has been around the longest – the separation of corporate and private morality. We discussed this in the opening section of this chapter. As in many other aspects of the new ethical banking, the traditional acceptance by many people that they can make a distinction between their public and private lives needs to be challenged when it comes to ethical behaviour. The time worn clichés continue to ring out:

— 'They're all doing it.'
— 'It's a tough world out there.'
— 'If we don't take advantage someone else will.'
— 'Who's going to find out?'

These assumptions must be challenged and replaced by new thinking and behaviour. What is needed is a clear definition of canons of ethical banking. Guidelines, not more laws, are what is required.

3.7 THE CONCEPT OF CANONS OF ETHICS

Banking is about lending – which calls for judgement and evaluation of consequences. Banking is about ethical behaviour – which also calls for judgement and evaluation of consequences. Down the centuries bankers have devised a methodology to guide their judgement in lending – the canons of lending. The very word 'canon' is borrowed from Christian dogma and has an ethical flavour. The basic canons of good lending state that before reaching a decision on a lending proposition the banker must be satisfied on seven counts:

(1) The character of the borrower.
(2) The ability of the borrower to repay.
(3) The margin of profit which will acrue from the loan.
(4) The purpose for which the loan is needed.
(5) The amount of the loan.
(6) The repayment arrangements.
(7) The security which will be realised if the loan is not repaid.

What is now needed is a set of canons to assist bankers in judging the ethical propriety of situations, particularly those involved in striving to meet the needs and expectations of customers, and in behaving ethically.

Ethical banking requires that a banker should establish a relationship with a customer which enables the needs of the customer to be met in a manner which:

— is within the law;
— fairly balances the interests of both parties;
— does not wantonly damage the legitimate interests of other parties affected by the banking relationship;
— can be justified, if required, to shareholders, employees, customers and others having a legitimate interest in the affairs of the bank;
— respects the confidentiality of the customer's affairs.

These five canons need to be followed as assiduously as the canons of lending.

The canons of ethical banking provide a template against which you can judge your behaviour when faced with an ethical dilemma. The watchwords are:

• Legality
• Fairness
• Social legitimacy

- Justification
- Confidentiality

These attributes will not restrict banking business. On the contrary, their acceptance by all concerned will lead to extended business as managers and staff feel secure in developing new types of client relationships.

3.8 LEGALITY

Banking and law have always been closely intertwined. In all developed countries there is a significant part of legislation exclusively devoted to banking and financial services. This is likely to increase, particularly in Western Europe as the Single Market develops.

In broad terms, legislation on banking falls into five categories:

(1) Laws relating to the setting up and viability of a bank or financial services company.
(2) Laws governing the taking and safeguarding of deposits.
(3) Laws controlling the types of activities in which a bank may engage.
(4) Laws safeguarding the rights of customers.
(5) Laws ensuring the resolution of disputes.

The report of the Review Committee on Banking Services Law (the Jack Report 1989) presages a new framework of law in the 1990s which will cover such matters as:

(a) The banker's duty of confidentiality.
(b) Cheques and analogous payment orders.
(c) Negotiable instruments.
(d) New technology.
(e) The plastic revolution.
(f) Countermand and completion of payment.

The implications of the new legislation for ethical banking are discussed in Chapter 6.

3.9 FAIRNESS

At first sight the canon of fairness may appear a theoretical concept, but this need not be so. Fairness usually refers to the terms of a transaction between people. A transaction occurs when two parties exchange something. For example, *A* gives *B* a pound, *B* gives *A* a melon. Since the transaction is voluntary it is reasonable to assume that both parties will benefit. The melon is worth more than a pound to *A* (otherwise he would not buy it), less than a pound to *B* (otherwise he would not sell it).

In any economic transaction there is a 'reserve price' for both buyer and seller. For the buyer it is the most he would have paid, for the seller it is the least he would have accepted.

The 'surplus' from any transaction is the difference between the buyer's and seller's reserve prices. In the melon example, if these reserve prices were £1.20 and 0.80p the resulting surplus would be 0.40p. Economists would argue that exchange will occur only if there is a positive surplus – in other words, the buyer's reserve price exceeds the seller's. Whenever an exchange does occur the total surplus is divided between buyer and seller. In the melon example, the surplus was allocated equally, both parties 'receiving' 0.20p or 50 per cent of the total.

Using the concepts of reserve price and surplus 'a fair transaction' can be defined as one in which the surplus is divided (approximately) equally. It follows that the transaction becomes increasingly unfair as the division deviates further from 'equality'.

While this definition may hold good for the majority of simple economic transactions, it has to be modified in several respects in banking transactions. In addition to the 'reserve price' and 'financial surplus', fairness also comes into play in terms of:

— Conditions relating to the period of the exchange.
— Conditions relating to individual freedom of action.
— Conditions relating to self-esteem and social worth.

3.9.1 Period of Exchange

In those cases where the bank is the buyer and the customer the seller, i.e. savings and investments, there will be conditions relating to:

(a) Period of notice of withdrawal.
(b) Amount which can be/must be withdrawn at any time.
(c) Frequency of withdrawals.
(d) Penalties for deviations from the normal conditions.

It can happen that while the 'financial surplus' is fair, the conditions relating to withdrawal of savings or invested funds reduces the balance of the surplus unduly in the bank's favour.

Looking at the other side of the savings coin, loans may have attached to them 'unfair' conditions concerning the time period for repayment, especially penalties for early repayment.

Although in banking terms time and money are synonymous this is not necessarily so in the perception of customers. The new ethical banker has to be mindful of this in explaining the benefits of savings or loans.

3.9.2 Individual Freedom of Action

A distinctive feature of banking transaction is that they can restrain the freedom of action of individuals in ways unforeseen by customers, or at least not fully thought through by them.

The saver/investor can find that there is limited access to funds when they are needed. The borrower may find that ability to move house is restricted if the house is part of the security for the loan. Admittedly, these constraints can usually be eliminated for a price – but this further reduces the 'surplus', making the transaction appear less 'fair'.

3.9.3 Self-esteem and Social Worth

These concepts come into play in seeking to establish the *intrinsic* values of a banking transaction. When the transaction is significant in the perception of the customer, for example, investing redundancy payments or buying a house, there are a number of forces at work which influence the view of 'fairness'.

The manner in which a customer is handled during and subsequent to the transaction can increase or reduce his/her evaluation of the 'psychic reserve price' and the 'psychic surplus'.

The psychic reserve price is the emotional level below which the customer will withdraw custom regardless of the 'financial reserve price and surplus'. There are four psychological factors which determine the psychic reserve price:

— Self-esteem
— Anxiety
— Confidence
— Comfort (both physical and emotional)

If the customer feels that self-esteem is being damaged because of the conditions of a loan, or feels that he/she is not being treated appropriately as a large depositor, the psychic surplus is reduced.

Similarly, where the customer is made to feel anxious about conditions attached to a loan, or is uncertain about the outcome of a decision which is long in coming, the psychic surplus is thus devalued.

Comfort, whether in the sense of pleasant surroundings or being put at ease is the fourth factor to which the new ethical banker must devote attention. When a transaction reduces the comfort level of a customer the chances of retaining that customer are also reduced.

3.9.4 The Fair Surplus

In ethical banking we should consider a fair surplus to have three components:

(1) The financial component, in terms of interest rates, fees, potential returns.
(2) The conditions component, in terms of obligations imposed on the customer.
(3) The psychic component, in terms of how the customer is made to feel during the transaction and throughout the ensuing relationship.

By astute application of the canon of fairness to each of the components, the banker can optimise the return on the financial surplus and still satisfy customers' desire for fairness by slightly exceeding their 'reserve conditions price' and 'reserve psychic price'.

3.10 SOCIAL LEGITIMACY

The canon of social legitimacy states that 'the relationship between banker and customer will not wantonly damage the legitimate interests of other parties affected by the banking relationship'. This canon, possibly the most controversial, reflects the need for bankers to be increasingly sensitive to the social consequences of their decisions. This does not imply a previous lack of social sensitivity; rather it suggests that a more rigorous approach to the social consequences of financial decisions will be called for in the future.

This could mean that monies invested by customers who have a declared opposition to certain activities should not be loaned to such activities. While the onus is on the customer to declare his/her antipathies when depositing funds, the new ethical banker should make the customer aware that their wishes will be respected (see section 4.7 in Chapter 4 on Customer Power).

Equally, it could be argued if a loan is going to be used to fund an activity which will be harmful to the environment, the ethical banker should not sanction such a loan. I am referring here to situations which will be recognised by the community affected and by society generally, as being socially harmful, such as a chemical plant emitting obnoxious fumes. The personal prejudices of a banker should *not* be used by themselves as a basis for judging the legitimacy of a course of action. That would be unethical.

3.11 JUSTIFICATION

Unlike the preceding canons, that of justification does depend solely on personal judgement. The canon states that any course of action can be justified, if required, to shareholders, employers, customers and others having a legitimate interest in the affairs of the bank.

Quite simply, the test is, would I feel ashamed if word of this got out? If the answer is yes, or even maybe – don't do it.

3.12 CONFIDENTIALITY

Confidentiality is no new phenomenon in banking. Yet it is interesting to note from the Barclays Charter (p. 61) that there was felt to be a need to give customers a reassurance on this subject in 1990. It will also be covered by new legislation arising from the Jack Commission and discussed in Chapter 6.

3.13 CONCLUSION

Ethics in banking are not a special type of ethics but are related to personal and social values. Businesses in general are becoming conscious of the importance of stimulating ethical awareness in management decision-making. This is in part the outcome of:

- Moral relativism;
- Acceptance of ethical erosion;
- The corporate mean of mediocrity;
- Short-termism;
- Separation of corporate and private morality.

Banking needs to follow its approach to establishing canons of lending by adopting canons of ethical behaviour which cover the fundamentals of:

(1) Keeping within the spirit as well as the word of the law.
(2) Being fair.
(3) Safeguarding the legitimate interests of others affected by a financial decision.
(4) Being able to justify your action.
(5) Maintaining confidentiality.

4 The Ethics of Customer Relationships

4.1 INTRODUCTION

Not all bank customers are honest; a number are unethical. Dishonesty ranges from robbery to lying about income on a loan application. The consequences of dishonesty in banking can be catastrophic leading to losses of millions of pounds, broken careers and damaged reputations. It is therefore understandable that bankers are brought up to be wary and disinclined to give the benefit of the doubt. Yet the essence of banking is risk-taking, so since time immemorial banks have confronted dilemmas of trust and risk assessment.

Technology is now at hand to assist, and increasingly replace, the financial risk assessment of a proposition, but the human and environmental aspects still rely wholly on human judgement.

The role of banker is shifting from lender to counsellor and with that there is a need for a reappraisal of the nature of banker–customer relationships.

4.2 BALANCED CUSTOMER RELATIONSHIPS

Customer relationships in banking have three unique features. The first is that a customer approaches a banker in one of four modes:

— a provider of money
— a borrower of money
— a transactor
— a seeker of advice and/or services

The second unique feature is that the relationship is one of reciprocal obligation. The third is that for the customer there is an 'aureole effect' surrounding each product or service. For example, what is a loan in the view of the banker, may for the customer be the chance to enjoy the countryside by having a car. We shall return to this later.

Let us first consider the four customer modes. In each mode the same customer brings to a situation a different mind-set in which preoccupations and perceptions differ.

The 'provider' mind-set is characterised by:

— high self-esteem;
— an awareness of options;
— a sense of creating an obligation vacuum which may need to be filled at a later date;
— a desire for the best deal.

The framing of the banker–customer relationship needs to be formed in a manner which responds to these characteristics while securing the best deal for the bank. This may mean that in negotiations (whether formal or at a subconscious level) the customer's preoccupation is focused on bolstering self-esteem rather than securing the highest rate of interest. An invitation to the local Institute of Bankers' Dinner can be worth more than an extra 1 per cent interest on an investment.

The 'borrower' mind-set will depend on whether the customer perceives the bank as first choice or last resort. Assuming the latter, the characteristics which predominate will be:

— low or damaged self-esteem;
— an awareness of lack of options;
— a sense of obligation;
— a willingness to complete a deal on terms dictated by the bank.

There will be a preoccupation with satisfying the bank manager. This can lead to exploiting the 'obligation vacuum' by persuading the customer to take on additional commitments. For example, the customer may feel 'forced' to buy an insurance policy or even a credit card to get the main loan being sought. We will be returning to the ethics of this type of behaviour.

The 'transactor' mind-set is much simpler than the others since it is likely to relate to a one-off transaction or a series over a long period. In most transactions the customer is preoccupied with reliability and speed. Customers in the transactor mode may use a bank for a variety of needs ranging from cashing cheques to paying bills, from using security boxes to sending money halfway across the globe. In money transmission the bank is perceived as a provider of a service which in fact may depend on a different industry – telecommunications. The ethical issues here are likely to cluster round justifying margins for acting as little more than a post box, supplying reassurances, keeping promises, complying with reasonable expectations of competence. Money which the customer is paying to be sent to Paris, Texas, should not arrive in Paris, France. This is an ethical issue in so far as the customer will have been led to assume that staff employed in money transmission have a basic knowledge of geography.

The 'seeker' mind-set can take many forms depending on the nature of the service or advice being sought. Furthermore, it can happen, particularly in corporate finance, that the customer is more knowledgeable than the banker. Omniscience is not a human characteristic; bankers should not feel ashamed to admit that they do not have it. Yet, it is a lack of willingness to own up to ignorance that can lead to customers being given the wrong advice or sold the wrong product.

The line between employing business acumen and taking advantage of ignorance is a fine one. But it is one that the banker crosses at his peril if the aim is to sustain a viable customer relationship. This means that bankers must be trained to identify the dominant mode in which a customer is operating and be capable of empathising. When modes are combined we see that there are nine possible types of customer.

- Provider
- Provider/Transactor
- Transactor/Seeker
- Borrower
- Borrower/Transactor
- Borrower/Seeker
- Transactor
- Provider/Seeker
- Seeker

In each mode there are 'ethical traps' which should be anticipated and avoided. These are listed in Table 4.1. Before considering the implications of these ethical traps we need to consider the other unique features of banking which were mentioned earlier in the chapter: the principle reciprocal obligation and the aureole effect.

4.3   THE PRINCIPLE OF RECIPROCAL OBLIGATION

Whenever a customer deposits money or borrows it a relationship of reciprocal obligation is established between customer and bank. In the provider mode, the customer expects the bank to safeguard the money invested and to increase its value through paying interest. In return, the bank expects the customer to leave the amount on deposit

Table 4.1 Ethical traps

Customer mode	Possible traps
Provider	Offering low rates without compensating benefits. Purposely withholding information on rate changes and other changes of benefit to the customer. Limiting options to disadvantage of the customer. Withholding information on conditions which could have a detrimental effect on the customer. Using jargon when clearer language would suffice.
Borrower	Charging excessive rates, arrangement fees, cancellation fees. Taking excessive security which limits further borrowing power of the customer unnecessarily. Giving the customer 'forced choice' of services/products the customer does not need. Allowing financial overcommitment by a customer without warning. Withholding information on rate changes and other changes of benefit to the customer. Limiting options to the disadvantage of the customer. Withholding information on conditions which could have a detrimental effect on the customer.
Transactor	Excessive charging for minimal service. Failing to follow customer's requirements without warning. Failing to compensate customers for damage caused by avoidable error. Limiting options to the disadvantage of the customer. Failure to admit responsibility for mistakes which have damaged customer.
Seeker	Recommending an adviser without checking bona fides. Recommending a service/product which is not in the costumer's best interests. Giving advice based on very limited knowledge. Failing to forewarn the customer of possible adverse repercussions of their proposed course of action. Taking advantage of adversity affecting the customer. Taking advantage of ignorance of the customer.

for the agreed period and to withdraw it in amounts and at times agreed at the outset of the relationship.

Similarly, in providing loans the bank expects the customer to repay in amounts and within time-spans agreed at the outset. The same concept of reciprocal obligation applies to mortgages, life assurance and other financial products and services.

An increasing amount of legislation surrounds customer–bank relationships; the vast majority of banks and their customers comply with these laws. Those who transgress the law are likely to be dealt with by the legal process. Fraud is a crime; unethical behaviour is not.

There are many aspects of customer–bank relationship which depend on the moral basis of reciprocal obligation rather than the legal basis. Furthermore, too strict an adherence to the word of the law rather than its spirit can lead to behaviour bordering on the unethical. Care can be taken to avoid falling into the types of ethical traps outlined in Table 4.1. Later in this chapter we will consider the ethical obligations of customers.

4.4 THE AUREOLE EFFECT

Medieval painters wishing to convey to the viewer that a particular figure on their canvas represented more than an ordinary human being surrounded the figure with an aureole or ring of light to signify saintliness. Similarly, a bank customer looks on a loan, overdraft or investment as having a distinctive characteristic which sets it apart from other products such as a cake of soap or a bar of chocolate. The aureole may be a sense of relief or of security, an opportunity to fulfil a lifetime's ambition, a saving from failure. Whatever it is the banker needs to see that aureole as well as the product.

4.5 ETHICAL TRAPS

These fall into two categories, like sin: traps of omission and traps of commission. Traps of omission normally relate to withholding information from the customer which could be of disadvantage to him/her; failure to keep the customer informed of options or changes which could be of benefit. Traps of commission include deliberately giving advice or selling products which are not in the best interest of the customer.

4.5.1   Traps of Omission

Listed below are eight traps of omission:

(1) Offering low rates of interest to investors without compensating benefits.
(2) Purposely withholding information on interest rate changes and other changes of benefit to the customer.
(3) Limiting options to the disadvantage of the customer.
(4) Withholding information on conditions which could have a detrimental effect on the customer.
(5) Failure to follow customer's requirements without warning.
(6) Failure to compensate customers for damage caused by avoidable error.
(7) Failure to admit responsibility for mistakes.
(8) Failing to forewarn customers of possible adverse repercussions of their proposed courses of action.

(1) *Offering low rates of interest to investors without compensating benefits*. Traditionally, banks offer a trade-off to depositors of higher interest rates for longer periods of notice to withdraw from the account. A bank manager has a duty to maximise deposits at the lowest rates of interest. There is nothing unethical about that. What is unethical is to offer the customer a lower rate than that available within the manager's discretion and to provide no compensating benefits such as financial planning advice, help in resolving financial problems which may seem major to the customer but are an everyday occurrence to the bank. This does not mean customers should invariably be offered the highest possible rates of interest for their savings. Lower rates acceptable to the customer should, however, be accompanied by some compensating benefit if the five canons of the new ethical behaviour are to be complied with. Lack of some compensating benefits is contrary to 'fairly balancing the interest of both parties'. It would also be difficult to justify to the customer, if challenged.

(2) *Purposely withholding information on interest rate changes and other changes of benefit to the customer* sins against the canons of fairness and justification. It is ethical to phase the timing of communicating, say, rises in rates for investors or other changes in policy and practices, if we genuinely believe that a customer would not be interested in them. For example, a person may want to keep on

current account a larger amount than is necessary to fund their cash needs. Providing they have been made aware of the fact that they are forgoing higher rates of interest, it is ethical to comply with the customer's preference. However, when knowledge of beneficial change is deliberately withheld this is not only inconsistent with the canons of fairness and justification, it could damage a third party, for example, potential heirs. Such acts of omission, therefore, lessen the social legitimacy of the relationship. In other words, it does not conform to best banking practice.

(3) *Limiting options to the disadvantage of the customer* is unethical in so far as customers are led to believe that the bank will look after their best interests. This does not mean that the banker has a duty to advertise competitors' products, but it does mean that the full range of products/services available from the bank with which the customer has chosen to do business should be made available to that customer. Unfortunately, bank managers and their staff can, under pressure, entice customers to purchase some 'products of the month', keeping alternatives hidden until they have reached their sales target.

(4) *Withholding information on conditions which could have a detrimental effect on the customer* is unethical when it leads to the creation of expectations which will not be fulfilled. Typical examples are:

(a) where a bank imposes a charge for a service without forewarning the customer;

(b) penalty payments for early repayment of loans are imposed without warning;

(c) limits on the timing and amount of withdrawals from savings are not explained at the time of opening the account.

Such practices are contrary to the canons of ethical banking.

It is, of course, the duty of the customer to read and understand the conditions covering relationships with the bank. But as these become more complex there is a moral obligation on the part of the banker to ensure that the customer is aware of the conditions, or is advised to seek legal advice before entering into a contract.

(5) *Failure to follow customers' requirements without warning* is unethical. Not only is it a breach of trust and may be unlawful, but it also offends the other canons. It may be that it is not possible to comply with customers' requirements and some minor changes may be necessary, e.g. sending a fax instead of telephoning. The ethical

dimension comes into play where deliberate action is taken or not taken and which has detrimental effects on the customer or a third party. For example, if a customer requests that money is transmitted in the fastest way possible and is charged accordingly, it is unethical behaviour to delay the transaction until there are sufficient similar orders to be despatched, thus incurring a lower cost. It is not unethical to select whichever transmission method the banker thinks fit if the customer has left it to his/her discretion.

(6) *Failing to compensate customers for damage caused by avoid-able error* is unethical, since it does not meet the canons of ethical behaviour and is contrary to the concept of reciprocal obligation. This trap needs to be considered under three types of damage:

— Financial
— Psychic
— Social

Financial damage is the easiest to assess and it is likely that some policy on such compensation will exist even if that policy is 'no compensation will be paid'. This is ethical providing steps have been taken to ensure that the conditions are legal and that the customer has been aware of such conditions at the time of the initial contact.

Psychic damage is likely to affect one's self-esteem and is more difficult to measure. For example, returning a cheque to drawer when there are adequate funds in the account may cause the customer little financial damage, but considerable upset because of the perception created in the receiver of the cheque. Psychic damage can be treated with psychic compensation; letters of apology or phone calls to the customer and others involved may suffice, provided swift action is taken to contain the damage.

Social damage to the standing and reputation of the customer may require both financial and psychic compensation. Much depends on the position of the customer and the nature of the problem. It is unethical for a bank to walk away from damage it has caused. By having an ethical code which recognises compensation in psychic and social terms, as well as financial, it is likely that levels of financial compensation will be lower than would otherwise be the case.

(7) *Failure to admit responsibility for mistakes* which have damaged a customer is unethical since it is contrary to the canons of fairness and justification. Like the preceding trap the damage may be financial, psychic or social. I am not suggesting that bankers should

be prepared to declaim a litany of sins or misdemeanours. Often all that is needed is a simple 'sorry'. It may be that some customers will take advantage of such honesty to make unjustified claims against the bank for excessive compensation. It is therefore ethical and prudent for the bank to have in place a procedure for handling mistakes and to make this clear to its customers. Obviously, the Banking Ombudsman (see Chapter 6) is part of the established complaints process for banks generally. But the vast majority of mistakes can be rectified and complaints handled at branch level if ethical banking has been properly implanted. How this should be carried out is the subject of Chapter 8.

(8) *Failing to forewarn customers of possible adverse repercussions of their proposed courses of action* is not only unethical but unwise, since it may lead to a loss of money and custom. Customers have the right to assume that bankers are more knowledgeable than themselves in matters of financial planning. Where the customer seeks guidance on such matters there are three courses open to the banker:

(1) State the limitations of knowledge on the subject, giving advice within those limitations and offering to provide or recommend a specialist adviser should the customer so wish.
(2) Imparting an impression of a greater depth of knowledge than is the case, giving the customer advice without the offer of referring the matter elsewhere.
(3) Giving advice based on an adequate basis of knowledge for the customers' needs, but withholding information on potential dangers in the recommended course of action.

The first approach is ethical, the other two are unethical since they are against the canons of fairness, legitimacy and possibly, legality. Once again, there can be circumstances where the customer does not provide the banker with accurate information. We shall deal with the obligations of the customer later in this chapter. Having covered the traps of ommission, we now turn to their equally unethical counterpart, traps of commission.

4.5.2 Traps of Commission

Commission is used in this context to describe acts which are committed, not charges which are levied. Using Table 4.1 as our reference point there are eleven traps of commission:

(1) Using jargon when clearer language would suffice.
(2) Charging excessive rates, arrangement fees, cancellation fees.
(3) Taking excessive security which limits further borrowing power of the customer unnecessarily.
(4) Giving 'forced choice' of services/products the customer does not need.
(5) Allowing financial overcommitment by a customer without warning.
(6) Excessive charging for minimal services.
(7) Recommending an adviser without checking bona fides.
(8) Recommending a service/product which is not in the customer's best interest.
(9) Giving advice based on very limited knowledge.
(10) Taking advantage of adversity affecting the customer.
(11) Taking advantage of ignorance by the customer.

(1) *Using jargon when clearer language would suffice* is contrary to the canon of fairness. It also conflicts with the concept of reciprocal obligation since the customer is placed at an undue disadvantage. It is ethical to use banking and legal jargon when no other forms of words are acceptable. But even when jargon has to be used the bank should take steps to ensure that the customer is aware of the vernacular for the words used.

(2) *Charging excessive rates, arrangement fees and cancellation fees* is unethical. It is ethical to charge different customers variable fees for similar services providing the basis of differentiation meets the canon of justification. For example, fees may be lowered to attract customers or in recognition of the volume of business produced by a customer, or as part of a sales drive.

(3) *Taking excessive security which limits further borrowing power of the customer unnecessarily* is unethical in terms of fairness, social legitimacy and possibly justification. While adequate security for certain types of loan is essential, where the security is excessive (for example, a first charge on a house worth £200 000 for a loan of £15 000) it unbalances the fairness element and can prevent a third party from providing finance which the customer may require.

(4) *Similarly, giving the customer a 'forced choice' of a services/ products* which he/she does not need is unethical in terms of fairness and can also affect legitimacy should a third party be prevented from offering a superior product through the action of the bank. This trap is widening as banks diversify into other areas of financial services

such as holiday and life assurance. Where a bank brings moral pressure to bear on customers to purchase holiday insurance as a 'condition' of extending the overdraft limit for the holiday period, or to purchase an endowment policy in order to receive a loan, there is scope for unethical behaviour if the specific needs of the customer for insurance or life assurance can be better met elsewhere. It can be argued that the customer has a choice and can take the business elsewhere. Exercising that choice can be burdensome if the customer has a variety of accounts, standing orders, direct debits and other services. The 'hassle factor' in moving accounts is considerable and can therefore influence the tolerance level of the customer for going along with unethical behaviour. In terms of long-term profitability, this ethical trap of 'forcing' unwanted or inappropriate products on customers produces negative financial results. After a time, particularly when the immediate financial need has been met, the customer is likely to abandon the additional unwanted products. Persistency rates (the maintenance of a policy) fall and the costs of setting up the policy, plus broker commission, means that no profit accrues to the bank. The loss of profit is likely to be compounded by a loss of customer goodwill.

(5) In much the same manner, the ethical trap of *allowing financial overcommitment by a customer without warning* of the danger can lead to financial losses for the bank. Once again, sound ethics result in a sound business outcome, unethical behaviour leads to an unsound business.

Examples of unethical behaviour by a bank which can lead to financial overcommitment are:

— Encouraging the use of credit cards by individuals who have no experience of managing their finances or have a poor track record.
— Giving ambiguous references on a customer to other providers of finance who will proceed to make loans at excessive rates.
— Taking insufficient time to gain and interpret relevant facts. (For example, an employer's reference which confirms that Mr X has been employed with the company for twenty years and has a salary of £20 000 can be less than helpful if it does not mention that Mr X is about to be made redundant.)

It is not unethical to use one's marketing skills to persuade customers to purchase new products. Indeed, as competition increases, the pressure to increase sales will also grow. What is unethical is knowingly to get a customer into a financial situation which can only be resolved by damage to himself and his creditors. (Knowing the resistance of some bankers to undertake a selling role, it is perhaps appropriate to remind reluctant sellers that it would be unethical to use this or any other trap as an excuse for not giving of their best in pursuing their sales targets!)

(6) *Excessive charging for minimal service* is treated separately from the earlier trap covering excessive rates, arrangement fees and cancellation fees. The reason for the separation is that the rates and other product-related charges are likely to be fixed centrally, whereas charges for many services will be left to local discretion. Such services can range from providing a written reference to arranging for the distribution of proceeds from a will, to providing night safes. All these services take time. It is ethical that the charges made should cover the costs of the time involved plus an element for the provision of particular expertise and, where appropriate, the use of equipment such as photocopiers and fax machines. Charges become unethical where all the costs are covered to an extent which is contrary to the canon of justification. It is ethical to charge more for superior service and/or high quality facilities. No hard and fast rules can be laid down, but a simple test would be for the banker to ask: if I was a reasonable customer would I feel that the charge for this service is justified; and would I accept the justification?

(7) *Recommending an adviser without checking bona fides* is an unlikely event but it can happen. Accountants, solicitors, computer services, printing services are all examples of professions and services which a customer new to the area might seek advice about from his banker. Sometimes there will be a temptation to recommend the person who has an account at the bank. There is no harm in this providing the service recommended is not knowingly inferior to that of another supplier who happens to be a customer of the rival bank. It is ethical to recommend customers providing there is the use of a caveat such as, this is the best supplier I know, but there could well be others as good or better if you want to enquire further. It is then up to the customer to pursue matters. The banker can take satisfaction in the knowledge that he/she has been ethical and at the same time may have contributed to better business for the bank if the customer–supplier proves satisfactory. Once again, sound ethics is synonymous with sound business.

(8) *Recommending a service/product which is not in the customer's best interest* is bad ethics and bad business. The points made earlier in relation to the 'forced choice' trap apply here also. In addition, there will be a widening credibility gap between the customer and the banker through which will ride triumphant competitors.

(9) 'A little learning is a dangerous thing' particularly when the 'beneficiary' of that knowledge believes that it is coming from a large reservoir rather than a muddy puddle. Therefore *giving advice based on very little knowledge, without admitting the limits*, is unethical since it offends the canons of fairness, social legitimacy and justification. It is unfair to the customer who is led to believe in the banker's professional skills; it could lead to damage to a third party such as business partners, employees, spouse; it would be difficult to justify giving the advice on such a shallow basis and without forewarning the customer. Ethical behaviour would involve admitting the limits of knowledge, giving the customer an opportunity to seek alternatives, seeking to improve one's knowledge if the customer decided to continue to use the banker as adviser.

(10) *Taking advantage of adversity affecting the customer* sounds such caddish behaviour that it may be difficult to conjure up the image of a banker who would indulge in such a practice. Unfortunately, it can happen that times of misfortune for a customer can provide opportunities for good fortune for the bank. The death of a spouse resulting in the sale of a house, the proceeds of which will be invested; redundancy payments which will be needed over a long term; compensation for a severe accident which will become the sole source of income. These are but examples of situations in which people are vulnerable to exploitation. Ethical behaviour would call into play most of the points already made in this chapter. An additional factor would be 'image'. A bank which is perceived to have exploited misfortune will suffer severe damage to its reputation, especially in this era of mass communication. It is therefore essential in these circumstances to ensure that behaviour complies particularly with the canon of justification.

(11) Finally, *taking advantage of ignorance by the customer* might be thought by the cynic to be the essence of banking! Certainly there is nothing unethical in taking advantage of culpable ignorance. If a customer is unwilling to seek out better rates, superior products, more professional advice than that provided by his bank, there is no obligation on the banker to inform the customer of alternative

sources. However, when it is obvious to a banker that a customer through no fault of his/her own is ignorant on the matter under discussion, it is unethical to take advantage of the situation. It may be that, due to the ignorance of the customer, more time may need to be spent on the affair, more work may need to be done, more staff engaged in meeting the customer's needs. In such a situation it is ethical to charge additional fees; this is not taking advantage, it is simply reaping a just reward.

4.6 ETHICAL OBLIGATIONS OF CUSTOMERS

The canons of ethical banking apply to the behaviour of customers as well as bankers. It is reasonable for a bank to operate on the assumption that its customers will:

(a) Comply with the law.
(b) Be fair and honest in the information provided to enable a banker to reach an ethical decision.
(c) Avoid involving the bank in situations which wantonly damage the legitimate interests of third parties.
(d) Act in a manner which can be justified to the bank and other interested parties.
(e) Respect the confidential nature of customer–bank relationship.

In terms of ethical behaviour bank customers can be classified into six types in ascending order:

(1) Criminals
(2) Rule-benders
(3) Ignoramuses
(4) Innocents
(5) Compliers
(6) Reliables

Criminals are unfortunately increasing. In 1989, the London Business School conducted a survey, the findings of which were:

— Crime costs UK industry over £3 billion per year, more than half of which is due to cheque fraud.

— Computer fraud is estimated at £400 million per year but is probably much greater.
— £830 million is stolen by employees.
— Bribery accounts for £220 million.

Banks in the past have unwittingly helped criminals by being reluctant to make public, or even to each other, crimes which have been perpetrated on them. As a consequence, a number of laws have been introduced since 1985 to force banks to be more open in the fight against global gangsters, be they drug barons or terrorists. The most important new laws to counteract crime are described in Chapter 6.

Every bank has its own procedures for preventing criminal activities. It would be unethical for these to be disclosed. Unfortunately, it will be increasingly necessary for crime prevention drills to take place regularly in banks.

Rule-benders are not criminals. They are customers who, having a sound knowledge of banking legislation and regulations, seek to take full advantage of them to the extent of trying to persuade bankers to bend the rules. The ethical point here is where flexibility ends and rule-bending begins.

The canons provide guidance; if rule-bending requested or practised by customers offends or is likely to offend any of the canons it is unethical. On the other hand, if rule-bending simply circumvents an internal regulation established for administrative convenience it need not be unethical.

Next in line to the know-it-all rule-benders are the ignoramuses. These are the customers who claim not to understand relevant regulations even when they do. They are likely to take advantage of any situation which is to their benefit (e.g. being credited with the funds of another customer with the same name); they will be quick to complain if they perceive any matter to their disadvantage (e.g. being charged for a telephone call at top rates).

The key ethical point about ignoramuses is that they are purposely and selectively ignorant. They need to be confronted with their unethical behaviour, otherwise it may well spread into criminality. To allow that to happen without attempting to prevent it would be contrary to the canons of social legitimacy and justification.

Innocents are ignorant through no fault of their own. Age (young or old) nationality, intelligence level, lack of education, fear of dealing with banks are all just causes for ignorance. There is an ethical obligation on the banker to ensure that innocents are helped to understand the rules which govern relevant banking activities and the consequences of their actions. For example, an innocent may pay in a cheque and not allow time for it to be cleared before drawing on it, thus becoming overdrawn without agreement. The subsequent charges will come as a genuine shock to the innocent both financially and psychically. There is an ethical duty to ensure that either the innocent has been forewarned of this eventuality or is dealt with constructively in the case of a 'first offence'; not to do so is against the canons of fairness, justification and, if a third party is damaged, social legitimacy.

The education of customers will be a key task of ethical banking. This will call for enhancing communications skills and an imaginative use of videos and other media. If airlines were banks, passengers would be instructed in safety drills only once in their lifetime, if at all. No one is advocating that, like the airlines, banks educate customers every time; but just as for the airline passenger every journey is slightly different, so too for the bank customer. Investing, getting a loan, arranging a pension, requesting a bank draft, using an automatic teller, are all different 'journeys', each with a potential hazard for the first-time traveller. Banks are not restaurants; the fact that a customer has been coming to the same bank for years does not mean that he/she is totally familiar with how to order what is on offer. The Barclays Charter (Table 4.2) is an example of educating customers.

Compliers are those customers who keep to the rules, no more and no less. This may be due to personal preference or to a reluctance to ask for flexibility. These customers can be overlooked when new products are introduced. The ethical point about dealing with compliers is to make sure that they are getting the full benefits of being a customer. They should be made aware of options and at least given the choice of being more adventuresome in their dealings with the bank.

Reliables are the backbone of any bank and like the backbone they may remain unseen until there is trouble. Reliables comply with bank rules but go beyond a relationship that is simply rule bound. They seek 'personal service' and are willing to pay for it.

Innocents, compliers and reliables need to be nurtured. They should be made aware of what is expected of them in terms of reciprocal obligations, helped in meeting their part of the deal and given recognition for their efforts.

Table 4.2   The Barclays Charter

As a personal customer of Barclays we believe you will want to know how we treat the information we hold about you.

Barclays has been in business for over 200 years. We recognise that if we are to continue to be successful we must understand and consistently meet your needs.

The Barclays Charter is our guarantee to you that we recognise that a special relationship exists between you as a customer and us as your banker. We operate within a framework of honesty, loyalty, mutual trust and privacy.

WHAT WE DO WITH INFORMATION ABOUT YOU

All the information we have about you will be treated with the utmost confidentiality. We set out below how we handle certain important aspects of our relationship. Other than as outlined below, details of your personal or financial affairs will not be disclosed to anyone else outside the Barclays Group without your prior permission, unless we are bound by law to do so.

You may find it useful to use the bank's name as a reference – for instance if you wish to open a credit account with a shop. This is a practice which has grown up over many years and is of value to all the parties involved. If we are asked to provide a reference for you, we do not divulge any details concerning your account, but we give to another financial institution a general opinion as to whether we think you can meet the obligations in question.

OUR POSITION TOWARDS MARKETING MAILINGS

We will never disclose your name and address for use by any organisation outside the Barclays Group. However, we may from time to time send you information about services which we believe may be of interest to you. We do not send out general mailings other than when enhancements to our existing product range need to be brought to your attention. For instance, we may be able to negotiate favourable insurance packages or we may be able to offer you a discount on your next holiday. All services which we offer will be of high quality and good value.

If after receiving such offers you do not wish your name to be included in the future, you should write to our Database Marketing Section, Barclays Bank PLC, Personal Sector Marketing Department, Juxon House, 94 St Paul's Churchyard, London EC4M 8EH. We will seek to ensure that you receive no centrally despatched promotional mail.

WHEN YOU OPEN A NEW ACCOUNT OR WANT TO BORROW

If you open an account with us or ask us for credit, we will normally make a search against your name at a credit reference agency. These are organisations which help lenders to lend responsibly. They also play a part in

---

(continued on page 62)

Table 4.2   *continued*

---

ensuring that borrowers do not become overcommitted. (You yourself can enquire what information is held about you on payment of a small fee.)

We will not disclose to a credit reference agency that we are granting you credit unless we have your specific agreement.

Information about you will be disclosed by the credit registration agency only for the purpose of credit risk assessment.

If you ask us for credit, we base our decision on the assessment of your personal financial circumstances and your ability to repay. To help us reach a fair decision, we will often use a system known as credit scoring. This is an objective mathematical method of assessing risk. It is approved by consumer organisations and is widely used by banks around the world. The decision to give you a loan is unaffected by your race, sex or religion.

SERVICE QUALITY

We are committed to offering you a high quality service. We aim to meet your requirements the first time you ask. We will rectify any mistakes promptly and efficiently.

IF YOU NEED TO COMPLAIN

If you have a complaint and your branch manager is unable to resolve the issue then you should write to our Customer Service Unit, Barclays Bank PLC, 54 Lombard Street, London EC4P 3AH (Freefone 0800 282390). In the unlikely event that the dispute cannot be resolved there is a Banking Ombudsman independent of the banks whom you may contact.

From time to time it may be necessary to change the Barclays Charter which applies to our UK mainland customers. The latest version will be displayed in all our branches.

A major challenge for ethical banking is to define the ethical obligations of customers in a manner which is clear, positive and encouraging. A prototype code is given in Table 4.3.

4.7 CUSTOMER POWER

In the 1990s, customer codes will become commonplace. Without them it will be difficult for companies to influence customer power. There is a growing awareness by politicians that customer power can provide them with political power. The Conservative governments of the 1980s introduced a plethora of legislation designed to safeguard consumers rights and, perhaps unwittingly, to boost customer power.

Table 4.3   Our customer code

1. We subscribe to the canons of ethical banking. This means that we seek a relationship with you the customer which:
   - is within the law of all countries where we conduct business
   - is fairly balanced in the interests of you and ourselves
   - does not wantonly damage the interests of other parties affected by our relationship
   - can be justified, if so required, to those who have a legitimate interest in our relationship
   - respects within the law the confidentiality of information provided by you.

2. These are not empty words, they are a reflection of our intention to provide you with the highest standards of service and integrity in all our dealings. This will only be possible if you are willing to help us.

3. To ensure that our relationship optimises our mutual benefits we ask you:
   - to assist us in complying with relevant laws relating to all your dealings with us
   - to provide us with the fullest details of your needs, expectations and circumstances in requesting our services
   - to help us avoid causing needless harm or damage to other parties affected by action arising directly from any agreement between us
   - to cooperate with us in being able to justify to legitimate interested parties situations arising from our relationship
   - to help us, within the law, to safeguard the confidentiality of our arrangements.

4. We recognise that we have an obligation to keep you fully informed of policies and procedures relevant to our relationship. To this end we will provide you with explanatory documents and other opportunities to acquire knowledge which will help you to help us.

5. We ask you to take full opportunities to seek from us any information and help you may need on all matters relating to our relationship which we shall seek to ensure is long lasting and of benefit to all of us.

From the 1960s, starting with the Consumer Protection Act (1961, revised 1971), there has come into operation the following legislation:

Hire Purchase Act 1964
Trades Description Act 1968
Supply of Goods (Implied Terms) Act 1973

Consumer Credit Act 1974
Data Protection Act 1984
Consumer Safety Act 1978
Banking Act 1979
Sale of Goods Act 1979
Insurance Companies Act 1982
Supply of Goods and Services Act 1982
Financial Services Act 1986

As is shown in Chapter 6 this type of legislation is continuing to affect banking. Customer power will certainly receive a great boost should the Labour Party gain power in 1992–3 and implement the proposals of its Consumer and Community Review Group. These take quality of life and quality of service as the rallying call of the 'new customer'. If elected Labour will:

— Establish a Department of Consumer Affairs with a Cabinet minister to work with, and on behalf of, consumers.
— Fund and support local consumer councils, linked to consumer protection and environmental health departments, with real power to act – not only to protect the interests of the individual but, where appropriate, groups of people.
— Establish a Quality Commission which will 'not only spread the word about good practice in public services and provide fundings to back innovation and enterprise, but will also involve the consumer'.

The proposals continue: 'those who deposit their money in banks and building societies or take out insurance policies have a *right* [my italics] to a say in what happens to their cash. At present, individuals simply hand over their money and by doing so empower the already powerful . . . Why should there not be a class of company director to represent the interests of consumers, elected by them and accountable to them?'

The message is clear; customer power is here and is growing. Banks can either wait for a government to use customer power for its own ends or, by adopting and living by the canons of ethical banking, customer power can be used as a positive force from which both banks and consumers will benefit.

4.8 CONCLUSION

Customer relationships need to be based on the canons of ethical banking. In so doing it is necessary to take account of three unique features of customer relationships in banking:

(1) The four customer modes of provider, borrower, transactor, seeker.
(2) Reciprocal obligation.
(3) The aureole effect.

There are several ethical traps which the banker must avoid in dealing with customers. These can be classified as:

— Traps of omission
— Traps of commission

The principle of reciprocal obligation imposes ethical obligations on customers as well as their bankers. When it comes to compliance with this principle, customers can be classified as:

• Criminals
• Rule-benders
• Ignoramuses
• Innocents
• Compliers
• Reliables

A key task facing banks is educating customers in carrying out their ethical obligations. Unless banks take such an initiative it will be difficult for them to influence customer power.

5 The Ethics of Bank Marketing

5.1 INTRODUCTION

Computer departments were the fastest growing part of banks in the 1970s. Marketing departments were the fastest growing in the 1980s.

Competition from other banks, building societies and non-banks such as retail store charge accounts have led to bankers being forced to be salesmen. Many are uncomfortable with this role since it transforms them from being bestowers of largesse (loans) to seekers of favours ('Please buy my products').

A number of marketing experts were drawn into banks from other industries in order to beat the sales drum. Bankers have been trained in sales techniques which are also drawn from other industries. But as we have seen from Chapter 4, banking *is* different in many respects from other industries.

Perhaps where ethical banking most needs to assert itself is in the marketing function.

5.2 CLASSIFYING CUSTOMERS

Traditionally, banks have segmented customers in terms of the traditional market research approach which classifies people in terms of their occupations from A (bishops) to E (pensioners). These classifications are becoming less relevant in the changing society of today. Marketing specialists are seeking new ways of targeting customers based on their expenditure patterns and lifestyles. These provide indicators of customers' needs and expectations.

When needs are not met or expectations are unfulfilled there is a greater propensity to complain. A survey in 1989 by the Office of Fair Trading revealed a greater willingness by customers to take a tougher line on demanding their rights. Based on information from trading standards authorities and Citizens Advice Bureaux throughout Great Britain, the survey identified four different types of consumer:

66

1) Bulls – agressive and sometimes overestimate their rights.
2) Know-alls – think they know their rights.
3) Strugglers – do the right thing by writing and phoning, but get frustrated.
4) Mice – too timid to complain at all.

These types were found to relate to personality rather than social class. Another study carried out at the same time by the Henley Centre for Forecasting confirmed this break with the traditional customer classification. The Henley study divides people into 'active' and 'passive' consumers.

The active consumer is aware of customer power and believes in making his/her feelings known when buying goods and services. Other characteristics of active consumers are:

— Will complain loudly if they feel dissatisfied.
— Likely to be well educated but not necessarily young.
— Do not see shopping as a non-thinking automatic process, but want to be informed on the policies of companies with whom they deal.
— Will readily switch from brand to brand.
— Cynical about claims of green policies which are not backed by truly environmentally friendly products.

The Henley study considers that being an active consumer is a state of mind that has spread to over 50 per cent of British adults. The remainder are classified as passive consumers, 'meek mild couch potatoes' who do not believe in answering back and are unaware of their customer power.

Passive consumers perceive themselves as at the mercy of suppliers of goods and services, including banks. They can be taken advantage of by the less scrupulous. Biased towards the less affluent and people in the North of England, passive consumers need help from ethical banking, so too do the young and the old.

5.3 YOUNG CUSTOMERS

If banks are to continue to prosper young people need special attention. They need help in developing financial self-management skills and in understanding how banks can help them. A major study by the advertisers McCann Erickson (*The New Generation* 1989) plotted changes in the values and behaviour of young people (aged 15–25) throughout Europe from 1977 to 1987.

Of particular relevance to ethical banking is the identification of a new ethic among young people who will form the main core of customers in the 1990s. This new ethic is not straightforward materialism, but a 'new set of symbolic values, where consumption can demonstrate individuality, sophistication, savoir faire, self-confidence'. The traditional view of work and reward is 'changing from a sense of service, fulfilment or belonging to a new one concerned with the consumption of goods and services'.

The McCann Erickson study stresses that the 'young now are no more greedy or foolish than any other generation. They are not duped by consumerism; it underpins their value system.' Community concerns, honesty and care for others remain extremely important values such as health, the family and friendship still play a dominant part in their ethical code. Work is seen as a means to an end, not an end in itself.

Focusing on young people in Great Britain, as distinct from the rest of Europe, the study revealed a somewhat different emphasis. The spirit of Thatcherism took hold on those whose teenage years coincided with the regime of only one Prime Minister – a phenomenon not experienced by any older generation still alive in the 1980s. The values of the 'Thatcherite young' are oriented towards personal success through hard work and money. A third of those questioned wanted jobs in banking and financial services. 'They have short term goals and many are practical and materialistic. The overriding discovery was the feeling that money was the doorway to modern life and that to consume is to have worth.'

Compared with their mainland European counterparts, British young people placed less emphasis on friendship, love and the welfare state. The British see wealth as the route to happiness, sophistication and individuality.

By comparison with a similar survey held ten years previously, the 1980s' study found that young people generally are more opposed to divorce and homosexuality, but less worried at becoming drunk at a party. The comparison showed little change in overall morality, with more young people disapproving of taking soft drugs than in the preceding decade. Unfortunately, there was a marked increase in the number of teenagers who would consider petty shoplifting.

Young people in Britain in the 1980s could be divided into two broad categories: the New Wave (aged 15 to 19), and the Baby Boomers (20 to 25).

Baby Boomers were teenagers in the years of the last Labour government. They were found to be:

— more liberal;
— interested in closer relationships;
— interested in seeking fulfilment through happiness to a greater extent than the New Wave;
— keen on the three Hs – health, hedonism and humanity.

In contrast, the New Wave teenagers:

— wanted aid to the Third World cut;
— wanted immigration restricted;
— were less concerned about the environment;
— tended to be cynical and group-oriented.

Forty-three per cent of British teenagers surveyed had a bank account and 28 per cent had a building society account. Eight per cent used a credit card. Tables 5.1 and 5.2 summarise those aspects of the British survey.

The power of young bank customers has shown itself in the government's Student Loans Scheme in 1989. Threat of boycott forced all the major banks either to refuse to participate or withdraw at the eleventh hour.

Bank marketing appears to lack a strategy in relation to young customers. The concept of 'catch them young and they'll stay with you' is less valid when modern technology can enable customers to transfer to another bank with little hassle.

Ethical banking will raise such questions as:

(a) At what age do we want to attract young people?
(b) In what ways can we enhance their money management skills?
(c) What particular counselling skills do we need to help our young customers in financial matters?
(d) How best can we convey the positive role which banking plays in local, national and world development?
(e) How do we create realistic expectations on the part of young people who seek to make banking their career?

Table 5.1   What makes happiness for young people, 1987 (percentages)

	Males	Females	15–19	20–25
Good health	56	58	53	60
Happy family life	33	48	36	44
Money	34	23	27	31
Friends	24	26	33	20
Success	24	20	28	17
Fun	20	14	21	15
Love	10	19	12	17
Job security	18	11	14	16
Peace of mind	10	11	7	13
A nice home	6	10	5	11

Table 5.2   Financial experience of young people, 1987 (percentages)

	Males	Females	15–19	20–25
Bank A/C	58	54	43	66
Building soc. A/C	31	33	28	36
Credit card	20	19	8	29
Stocks/shares	8	3	3	8

(f) How do we refuse to open accounts for young people without causing hurt?

These issues once resolved will provide a more viable young people's market than any number of gimmicky promotions.

Applying the canons of ethical banking to young people (aged 15–25) should result in:

(1) An awareness in young people of the legal obligations of banks and customers ('Let's both keep to the rules').
(2) A recognition that banks operate in a spirit of fairness and expect this to be reciprocated ('If you've got a problem tell us straight away and we'll try to help').
(3) An awareness of social legitimacy in the activities of the bank, underlining the bank's involvement in social developments ('You are not the only ones who want to make a better world').
(4) A realisation that we are all accountable for our actions ('Whatever we agree has got to be justifiable').

(5) A respect for confidentiality ('If we make an exception in your case, please don't broadcast it').

5.4 OLDER CUSTOMERS

Turning from the young to the old, it has been calculated that by 1995 the generation in its forties in 1990 will inherit up to 35 per cent of all the houses in Western Europe from the generation now in its sixties. In Britain, £9 billion of assets will change hands through inheritance between 1990 and the turn of the century.

This inheritance will take the shape of not just housing but of consumer durables such as refrigerators, washing machines, televisions, plus jewellery, paintings and antiques. Many of those in their forties, however, already own goods of this sort. The result will be that the surplus goods will be passed on to the children of those now in their forties. This will have several consequences for banking:

— The demand for loans to purchase consumer durables will slow down.
— Manufacturers of consumer durables will be adversely affected.
— There will be an increasing demand for spares and repair services.
— The net worth of the 'chattels' of individuals will need to be brought into estimates of creditworthiness; alternatively, pawnbrokers will prosper.

In addition to manufacturers being spurred to produce products specifically designed for the older market, such as an easy-to-handle vacuum cleaner, service industries will have to respond to new needs. For example, 80 per cent of all luxury travel sold in the United States is purchased by people over 55.

Banks and other financial institutions will also need to anticipate the needs and expectations of their older customers. Ways of releasing the equity which retired people have tied up in their homes have existed for some time. Unfortunately, some of these schemes have had characteristics which are the antithesis of ethical banking.

More old customers will reside in retirement homes; bankers should be prepared to visit them in residence. Codes of conduct for such visits should be drawn up to avoid any charges of 'exploitation'. Similarly, bankers should discreetly monitor the financial affairs of older customers to ensure that they are not being exploited by others;

simple computer programmes can be set up for this. Longevity will present some of the major challenges for ethical banking.

5.5   THE THIRD AGE CUSTOMERS

In his book, *A Fresh Map of Life* (1989), Peter Laslett deals with the consequences of longevity. He argues cogently that the 75 plus age group will increase and that new needs will arise as lifespans extend into the nineties and centenarians become commonplace.

> Uncertainty about possible length of human life is of considerable symbolic significance for the elderly who live in a state of perpetual doubt . . . They cannot tell if they should cling on to their capital, and persist in habits of saving just in case, or if they should give away in their lifetimes, possessions as well as money, should money be at their disposal. (ibid.)

Laslett suggests that retirees under 75 (in their second age) are beginning to experience a number of fears about continuing into their Third Age. Although ethical banking cannot resolve all these fears, it will have to bear them in mind in seeking to meet the needs and expectations of older customers:

> First, is the fear of death; it is now almost exclusively the elderly who die.
> Second, is the fear of senile decay such as Alzheimer's disease.
> Third, is the fear of life-destroying, bed-enforcing diseases of decline such as cancer and heart disease.
> Fourth, is the fear of less life-threatening but grave afflictions such as blindness, deafness, lameness, incontinence.
> Fifth, is the fear of physical debility, mental decline and illness which increase their dependence on others.
> Sixth, is the fear of loss of beauty, attractiveness, fertility, potency.
> Seventh, is the fear of inability to recall names, events, people, experiences.
> Eighth, is the fear of loss of keenness of hearing, eyesight, and smell. (Together with the seventh fear this creates an apprehension of losing the capacity for enjoyment.)
> Ninth, is the fear of loss of mobility, of being confined indoors and of the consequent loss of choice of places to go and things to do.

Tenth, is the fear of loss of earning power.
Eleventh, is the fear of falling status, public status and private status within the family.
Twelfth, is the fear of loss of spouse, siblings, kin, friends, family and consequent desolation.
Thirteenth, is the fear of loss of home, having to live with other people or in an institution.
Fourteenth, is the fear of the contraction of the future, frustration in fulfilling the chosen plan of life. (ibid.)

Ethical banking can reduce the effects of many of these fears in a number of ways:

(a) Providing a range of insurance and saving products geared to the needs of the Third Age.
(b) Giving early financial advice.
(c) Making visits to a bank branch a pleasant, relaxed experience (e.g. toilet facilities should be made more readily available to older customers).
(d) Visiting the elderly and reassuring them on their financial situation wherever justified.
(e) Showing an understanding of their fears and helping with these where some financial solution is possible.

5.6 VALUES AND LIFESTYLES

The generations between the teenage New Wave and the elderly Third Age provide the majority of the personal customers of a bank.
 Since the mid-1960s research has gone into identifying distinctive lifestyles of individuals which provide insights into:

— Purchasing behaviour
— Product usage
— Media usage
— Activity patterns

Much of the research was conducted by the Stanford Research Institute, California and has been popularised by various authors.
 Known as the VALS (Values and Lifestyles) typology, this approach defines nine categories of stereotypes each of which shares

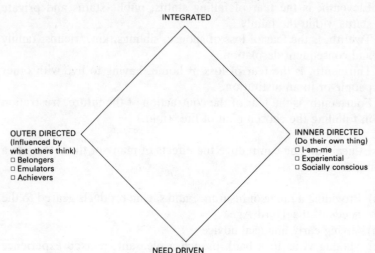

Figure 5.1   Typology of lifestyles

similar values. Figure 5.1 outlines the typology; the eight interrelated types, below the top integrated level, falling into three groups:

- the Need driven
- the Outer directed
- the Inner directed

In terms of ethical banking these groups can be responded to in various ways.

The Need driven are the 'money restricted' customers who are struggling just to buy the basic essentials. They buy more from need than from choice. Sometimes they go on a spending spree, buying luxury goods (often with credit cards) which they cannot afford. This group falls into two categories:

- Sustainers
- Survivors

Sustainers are relatively young, assertive, struggling on the edge of poverty, hard working and anxious to get ahead. They can be a profitable segment for small personal loans. A growing part of the

Sustainers subgroup is female single parents. Sustainers are more likely to be 'active' consumers.

Survivors, on the other hand, are more likely to be 'passive' consumers. They are the old, depressed, alienated poor – the underclass. How banks should respond to them is discussed in Chapter 7.

The largest group of consumers is the Outer directed. They make up the largest middle core of bank customers, conducting their lives according to what they believe other people will think of them; hence the term 'outer directed'.

There are three subgroups in the Outer directed category:

- Belongers
- Emulators
- Achievers

Belongers provide the mass market for banks. They are the backbone of the nation; traditional, conservative, conventional, unexperimental. Their lives revolve round their homes and families. They are members of the Women's Institute, British Legion, Rotary, and the like; people who would rather fit in than stand out – some might say 'your typical bank manager'.

Emulators live in a totally different style from the Belongers. They are trying to burst into 'the system' – to make the big time. Ambitious, upwardly mobile, status conscious, macho, competitive, they can be distrustful and angry with little faith that they will be given a fair chance by the establishment – some might say 'your typical corporate banker'. The archetypal Yuppie emulators existed long before that label was coined for the young upwardly mobile professional person in the 1980s; they will exist when the label is forgotten.

Achievers have made it, whether in business, professions, government; they are the leaders of the pack. Fame, the good life, status, comfort, competence are the distinguishing characteristics of the Achiever. These able and affluent people have a vested interest in maintaining the system which created them – some might say 'your typical merchant banker'.

The third category in the VALS typology is the Inner directed comprising three subgroups:

- I-am-me
- Experiential
- Socially conscious

Traditional bankers have been least comfortable with the Inner directed; the same will hold for the ethical banker. Fortunately, the latter can be helped to cope.

I-am-mes are young, impulsive, exhibitionist, fiercely individualistic and highly inventive. This is a segment of the market which British banks in the 1980s tried to capture with varying degrees of success. It is a fast changing segment, most of its members mature to Experientials or the Socially conscious.

Experientials are people who want direct experience and deep involvement. They are highly participative but also given to introspection. Their interests lie in Eastern religions, crafts, communes and new ways of living. They are not ideal bank customers.

The fastest growing subgroup throughout the Western world is the Socially conscious. They have a high sense of social responsibility, concerning themselves with environmental issues, disarmament, consumerism, and political freedom. Like other Inner directed they are active consumers. More than any other category they will prove a strong force in shaping the new ethical banking. As discussed in Chapter 2, it is this group which has influenced the growth of 'ethical investments'.

Finally, at the top of the VALS hierarchy stand the Integrateds. At peace with themselves and the world, these fortunate people are fully mature in a psychological sense, being tolerant, assured, self-aware, strategic thinkers – some might say 'the ideal ethical banker'.

5.7 RESPONDING TO LIFESTYLES

The influence of the lifestyle approach to matching customers' financial needs is reflected in the way in which bank products have been designed in the late 1980s. Money is being advertised for sale just like any other product; increasingly it is being 'branded'.

The Midland Bank has launched three 'branded accounts':

• Vector
• Meridian
• Orchard

Vector is designed for the Emulators; in the advertisement launching this brand the self-confident, young customer was shown to have a low respect for the bank manager. The customer is projected as an opportunist who wants what he can get out of the bank and does not see why he need 'grovel' for it.

The Vector product carries a £10 per month charge which allows customers to incur a 'free' £250 overdraft without receiving a 'nasty letter'. It is not a cheap product although to some it may appear to cheapen the banker–customer relationship. The advertising plays on the fears of customers being treated by the banker in a manner which calls for grovelling by the customer. It poses the parties in an adversarial position; it is contrary to the spirit of ethical banking.

The Meridian account is designed for the Achievers. It provides a full banking service for those who have money for investment. This account offers large discounts on home loans, but since most of the target customers are likely to have mortgages this may be seen by some as a cynical piece of marketing.

The Orchard account is for the mass market of Belongers; 'family-forming and home-owning groups', in the words of the Midland Bank. It is designed for spenders and savers who have mortgages, children, holidays and cars to pay for, as well as putting aside something for a rainy day.

The three brands, in a sense, define banker–customer relationships. The Vector brand is, despite the advertising, for those who want an arm's length relationship, because any closer proves to be uncomfortable. The Meridian is for those who know they can call on the manager at any time; he needs them more than they need him. The Orchard brand is for those who have a 'handshake' relationship with their manager.

5.8 THE ETHICS OF BRANDING MONEY

Sally Rowland, a researcher on Channel 4's *The Media Show*, has raised some issues about the ethics of this approach of 'branding' money (*New Statesmen and Society*, 4 November 1989).

> The message in the Vector commercials – and also to an extent in Credo ['I believe'], Midland's service aimed at small businesses – is that in a modern world of mistrust and confrontation . . . supreme and smart one-upmanship is the only way to get ahead . . . Throughout a crop of financial commercials there is a clear theme of personal choice and a total pre-occupation with the desires of the individual.

After analysing a range of advertisements from banks and building societies, Rowland suggests that: 'The cumulative effects of these commercials is to perpetuate an idea of easy money, quick to get hold of and easily disposed of . . . What the commercials . . . do is perpetuate a myth that money comes easy, and seductive "lifestyle" images are the acceptable norm.'

This advertising approach is seen as a contributor to the growing indebtedness of the young poor. Without venturing into a political stance, the question has to be asked if the advertising of easy money in times of historically high interest rates is in the best interests of banking. Advertising of bank products should be tested against, not only the words of the five canons of ethical banking, but also the spirit.

A similar test should be applied to market research.

5.9 THE ETHICS OF MARKET RESEARCH

Competitive pressures have forced banks to conduct market research to a far greater degree in the 1980s than in any previous decade. Two reasons for this trend are the amounts spent in advertising and the potential of the personal sector market.

At the beginning of the 1980s British banks spent just under £40 million annually on advertising. By the end of the decade this had grown to annual spending of £333 million and this is forecast to rise to £400 million in the early 1990s. Even allowing for inflation this is a substantial increase. However, there is a strong desire among banks to make sure that they are directing their message at the most profitable market segments.

By the end of the 1980s the personal savings sector accounted for £80 billion in bank accounts, £125 billion in building societies and £140 billion in life assurance. Any bank or financial institution that can increase its market share by even 1 per cent will profit significantly.

Traditionally, market research in banking has been conducted by questionnaires mailed to customers; spot check polls in the high street bringing together a randomly selected cross-section of adults to form a focus group. This last approach is being further developed and it raises questions for ethical banking.

The 1990s will see the growth of market research which seeks to probe the consumer psyche. Aware that one bank provides similar services to its competitors the key question will no longer be: *who* banks with us? but *why* do they bank with us?

Among the techniques coming into use are:

— Point of sale observation – customers' behaviour, reactions to sales offers and other conduct while in a bank branch are studied by trained observers, sometimes using closed circuit television.
— Projective techniques – customers are asked to describe banks as animals; to write 'obituaries' for their own bank and its main competitor.
— Humanising the inanimate – customers are asked to carry on both sides of the conversation with their bank. 'You are efficient, helpful, but lacking in affection,' might say the customer, replying, as the bank, 'Sorry, I'm going to smile a bit more in future.'
— Semiotics – the use of symbols in advertising to create a desired image.

More sophisticated techniques which are in use in other industries and are likely to spread to banking are the use of electro-encephalograms to measure how people react to parts of a TV commercial; the use of laser technology to see advertisements through the eyes of the consumer. For instance, Perception Research Services Inc., in the United States, used an invisible beam of light to monitor some hundred people as they read a prototype advertisement for Bombay Gin. The study found that nine out of ten people ignored the product's name. A revised layout boosted the recall level by almost 100 per cent.

A report in *Newsweek* quoted an example of the use of these techniques by an advertising agency seeking to gain the account of the financial giant Merrill Lynch, renowned for its symbol of a charging bull. The advertising agency called on the services of a veterinary psychologist to advise them of the ins and outs of bull behaviour'. A Bozell executive admits the tactic 'was a lark, but the firm *did* win the contract'. Which, in the words of *Newsweek*, 'perhaps just goes to show, in the brave new world of advertising research, a little bull can go a long way' (*Newsweek*, 27 February 1989).

While it has its humorous aspects, market research using techniques of which the customer is unaware is against the canons of ethical banking. Certainly, the customer is placed at an unfair disadvantage.

A more common technique which I believe is also unethical is the use of mystery shoppers. These are individuals recruited and trained by advertising agencies to pose as ordinary customers or potential customers in branches of the client bank and its competitors. Although this approach may yield useful competitive information and can help to monitor performance of staff against standards, it offends the canons of ethical banking on several scores:

(a) The mystery shopper is not a genuine customer and therefore the relationship between banker and mystery shopper is unjust.
(b) Attention to the needs of mystery shoppers diverts effort from serving genuine customers and is therefore not legitimate.
(c) When it is known that mystery shoppers are in use, bank staff may be diverted from observing security drills devised to deal with fraudsters and robbers. ('I thought he was behaving oddly but I assumed he was a mystery shopper.')

5.10   ETHICAL MARKET RESEARCH

Abiding by the canons of ethical banking will provide more useful research in the long term than the use of pseudo-scientific methods or paid informers otherwise known as mystery shoppers.

Market research methods which are ethical and effective are:

(a) Survey questionnaires sent to large numbers of customers which state clearly the purpose of the survey and provide opportunities for customers to comment on any issue.
(b) Comment cards at the counter in branches or included in cheque books, deposit slips or other documentation.
(c) Customer roundtables at which a cross-section of customers meet as a group and give their views on various topics.
(d) Open days or evenings when customers and others are given the opportunity to meet bank staff and voice their opinions.
(e) Freefone comments line for use by anyone who wants to express an opinion or make a complaint.

In every case, those involved are aware of what they are being asked to do. Their opinions and perceptions are being solicited without probing their psyche. They are being treated as rational human beings and not guinea pigs.

5.11 CONCLUSION

The customer base of banking is changing. This is partly due to demographic trends – fewer young people, more very old people – and to lifestyles. Customers are becoming more active in asserting their rights and in using customer power to influence company policies.

Recognising that there is a marked similarity in the products and prices of competing banks, each is seeking to differentiate by developing brands which are heavily advertised.

The growth in advertising costs has led to the adoption of a wide range of psychologically based market research. Some of this is of doubtful value and much of it is contrary to the canons of new ethical banking. Fortunately, there is a range of effective and ethically sound market research techniques available to the new ethical banker.

6 Ethics and New Banking Law

6.1 INTRODUCTION

The first canon of ethical banking states that 'a bank and a customer will conform to a pattern of behaviour that is within the law'. Like the other canons this may appear self-evident, were it not for the fact that there are frequent occasions when banks and customers are seen to break the law. Recent years have seen a spate of new laws ranging from the Financial Services Act of the mid-1980s to the impending Banking Services Act in the early 1990s.

The Review Committee on Banking Services Law under the chairmanship of Professor R.B. Jack published its far reaching report in 1989. The committee reviewed all existing banking Law and other statutes, such as the Unfair Contract Act 1977 and the Data Protection Act 1984, which have implications for bank–customer relationships. Among its recommendations the committee proposed a Code of Banking Practice to which banks and building societies should subscribe. The purpose of the code is 'to give guidance on the existing legal requirements and . . . to promote . . . desirable banking practices'.

6.2 CODE OF BANKING PRACTICE PROPOSALS
(A detailed code is due to be published in 1991)

Three principles govern the proposed non-statutory code and related legislation:

(1) There should be 'fairness and transparency in the banker–customer relationship'.
(2) Confidence in the security of the banking system should be maintained.
(3) 'A bank's duty of confidentiality to its customer, which is a special feature of the banker–customer relationship, should not be eroded.'

The proposed code is in three parts:

— Underlying aspects of the banker–customer relationship.
— Rules applying generally to the customer's account.
— Rules specific to electronic funds transfer.

What follows is a summary of the main points of the code together with my comments on its relationship with ethical banking.

6.2.1 Banker–Customer Relationships

• Banks should ensure that they can establish the identity of a person opening a new account. (This is in part to protect the bank from charges of dealing in illicit funds. It also is in line with the canons of legitimacy and justification.)

• In communicating to the customer the terms of a contract the bank should ensure that the customer is given a fair and balanced view of the terms and their implications. Any changes to the terms must be given with due notice. (This is in line with the canon of fairness.)

• Banks should establish internal procedures for handling customer complaints, (This accords with the canons of fairness and justification.)

• Banks should make clear to customers their procedures relating to confidentiality:

— Where disclosure is under compulsion by law;
— Where the interests of the bank require disclosure;
— Where disclosure is made by the express consent of the customer.
— Where there has been a breakdown of the banker–customer relationship arising through customer default.

(All five canons of new ethical banking come into play in this part of the code. The Data Protection Act of 1984 greatly increases the power of customers to gain access to their computer files. In this regard it is unethical to place on file any description of the customer which would be a cause for embarrassment, offence or legal action.)

• Banks should give all customers an explanation of their procedure for giving 'bankers' opinions' (references) to third parties. Customers should be encouraged to give or withhold a general consent or specific authority. Without such agreement banks should refrain from giving opinions unless compelled by law. (All five canons are covered. Care needs to be taken to ensure that opinions are not conveyed orally or even by body language, without the customer's consent. The question of passing internal opinions within departments of a bank or with its subsidiaries is unethical if the subsidiary advertises in a manner which implies it is autonomous.)

- Banks should exercise constraint in the direct marketing of their services. Customers should be made aware of the marketing purpose for which they are being approached. The banks should respect the wishes of customers who do not want to receive or be otherwise involved with direct marketing. (As competition increases there will be growing pressures within banks to use their customer data base to enhance sales. Ethical banking would suggest that customers be forewarned of this possibility and be given the opportunity to opt out of such schemes.)

The Barclays Charter (p. 61) incorporates most aspects of this section of the proposed code.

6.2.2 Customers' Accounts

- Banks should explain to customers the timing of the clearing cycle and the concept of cleared balances. (This accords with the canons of fairness and legitimacy. New ethical banking recognises the importance of customer education. The better informed customers are, the more confident they will be in using banking services. Furthermore, the incidence of errors and complaints arising from uninformed customers will decline.)

- Banks should give their customers an explanation of 'truncation' (the retention of cheques by the collecting bank which electronically transmits the payment information to the paying bank). Disputes arising from truncation which are not resolved within three working days should result in the customer's account being recredited pending final resolution. (This accords with the canon of fairness. It also exemplifies another concept of ethical banking which we have not raised until now – when there is ambiguity the customer should be given the benefit of the doubt.)

- A bank should not return within six months from the date of issue a cheque or bank payment order on the grounds that it is out of date. (This is an operational matter; its only implication for ethical banking is that customers should be made aware of the deadline.)

- Banks should explain the rights of bank and customer in regard to transactions effected by Bank Giro Credit. (Once again, this highlights the need in ethical banking for banks to provide more customer education than has been the case to date.)

- In using multifunctional cards customers should be free to select those functions they require. Non-selected functions should be blocked off. Should the card be compromised, the customer should (fraud on his part excepted) have no liability on any function he has not authorised. (This is in accordance with the canon of fairness and legitimacy. We see in this a shift to banks being held accountable for errors until they can prove otherwise.)

- Banks as card-issuers should inform all their customers who are cardholders of their rights and obligations in respect of loss or theft of cards. (The concept of reciprocal obligation comes into prominence here as it will increasingly in ethical banking.)

- A bank should advise its customers of the rules governing different payment systems, particularly what is involved in countermanding an instruction or authority. (This concurs with the canons of fairness, legitimacy and justification. Ethical banking needs to provide for customer education here as in other areas. The outmoded attitudes that customers do not need to know or would not be able to understand are giving way to a proactive approach to customer education.)

- Customers should be informed of the level of charges for services; they should be told what are the services for which they will be charged. (This is in line with the canons of fairness and justification. Ethical banking will, through such practices, force banks to perform to higher competitive standards to justify their tariff *vis-à-vis* their competitors.)

- Where a bank undertakes a foreign exchange transaction for its customer, it should ensure before completion that the customer is aware of all charges and the rate of exchange. (This concurs with the canons of fairness and justification. It widens the options for the customer seeking competitive rates and standards of service. If ethical banking is in operation it should reduce the likelihood of a customer receiving an unpleasant surprise at the charges made.)

- Banks should ensure that prospective guarantors are adequately warned about the legal and other implications and the importance of receiving independent advice. (The canons of legitimacy and justification are relevant here. In addition the concept of reciprocating obligation applies very forcibly to this type of activity.)

6.2.3 Electronic Funds Transfer (EFT)

This part of the recommended code of practice covers such matters as:

- Authentication of customers' instructions;
- Written records available to customers under the Data Protection Act 1984;
- Customers' right of action in disputes;
- Apportionment of loss arising from a disputed EFT.

6.3 BANKING SERVICES WHITE PAPER

In March 1990, the government issued a White Paper – *Banking Services: Law and Practice*. This was a response to the proposals outlined above; its aim is to strengthen customers' legal rights in such matters as:

— Bringing debit cards and other plastic cards within the scope of the Forgery and Counterfeiting Act 1981.
— Banning unsolicited mailing of all payment cards, i.e. debit and charge cards.
— Imposing a limit of £50 on a customer's potential loss if a debit card goes missing.
— Imposing a liability for losses that arise through a failure of a bank's electronic funds transfer equipment.

The code of practice proposed by the Jack Committee was accepted in principle by the government as a basis for a self-governing code to be devised by the British Bankers Association, the Building Societies Association and the Association for Payment Services.

The White Paper foreshadowed a stream of legislation and self regulation on banking matters which will flow through the industry in Britain in the 1990s. Added to this will be further legislation from the European Community.

As banks become more international they find themselves having to comply with a variety of laws. For example, the Yorkshire Bank, in addition to complying with British and Community laws, has to take full account of the laws of Australia (where its owner, the National Australian Bank, is based) and of the United States where other subsidiaries of the National Australian Bank operate. The more varied the legal systems involved, the greater is the need to have well-defined ethical standards and practices.

6.4 ETHICAL IMPLICATIONS OF NEW BANK LAWS

The recommended code of conduct summarised above is non-statutory. Nevertheless, it foreshadows likely trends in bank legislation. These can be summed up thus:

(a) Legislation will be biased towards customers' rights and banks' duties.
(b) In disputes the burden of proof will rest with the banks rather than the customers.
(c) Banks will be presumed to have 'educated' their customers to a much larger degree than before.
(d) Banks will be required to publish and justify their charges of all types for all their activities.
(e) Decisions to decline loans or refuse to provide services to certain customers will have to be justified to those concerned.
(f) Banks will be restricted in the amount of personal data which they can require from customers and how they use it.

It might be thought that with increased legislation there is less need for ethical banking – surely the laws will take care of everything? On the contrary, it would be a sorry and unprofitable day for banking if all facets of the bank–customer relationship were to be dictated by legislation rather than by ethical behaviour. Ethical behaviour is the oxygen which will enable the bank–customer relationship to breathe and develop on a person-to-person basis, rather than one based solely on sterile laws.

Each of the trends in legislation can be moulded by ethical banking to provide those banks willing to put in the effort and commitment with competitive advantage. This is because, as we shall see in Chapter 7, customers have distinctive needs, expectations, perceptions and mind-sets which do not lend themselves to the broad brush

88 *The Essentials of Ethical Banking*

of legislation, but need to be treated with the keen eye and sensitive touch of the miniaturist. Nevertheless, ethical banking will be influenced by the legislative trends listed below.

6.5 CUSTOMERS' RIGHTS AND BANKS' DUTIES

Providing customers with rights which are enshrined in legislation will give no bank a competitive advantage. What is needed is to anticipate what the legal rights will be and institute them before being forced to do so. This will mean the publication and adoption of a code of ethical conduct. Training in applying the code will be necessary for all employees. Transgressions of the code need to be identified and the transgressor punished.

Care needs to be taken to convey to managers and staff that adherence to the code is not a limitation on their powers, but a strengthening of their ability to serve. By making explicit aspects of behaviour which have not hitherto been discussed freely, ethical banking can help release energy which previously was used up in dealing with ambiguity and worry about doing the right thing.

By inculcating behaviour which responds to customers' rights in a positive non-defensive manner, there will be an increasing confidence in both customer and banker which should result in the generation of more business as customers become aware of all the services which a bank can provide.

6.6 BURDEN OF PROOF

As the law shifts the burden of proof in disputes from the shoulders of customers to those of bankers, it will be necessary for banks to have accurate and swift systems to provide the pertinent data. Practising ethical banking will reduce the opportunities of error since such behaviour engenders openness and trust. Furthermore, by empowering staff at customer-contact level to resolve disputes up to a certain financial ceiling this will save time and management energy.

Disputes can often be about psychic or social damage as much as financial loss. If staff are empowered to make amends not only financially, but by token gestures, ethical behaviour in line with the five canons will severely limit the damage caused by small claims from customers.

The prospect of laws for psychic hurt may be far off in Britain, but they are being actively debated in the United States. In February 1989, *Newsweek* reported on how two American lawyers used the concept of 'loss of happiness' to win large damage awards for accident victims. They have devised a mathematical formula for estimating what they call 'hedonic damages' (after the Greek word *hedone*, or pleasure).

Their goal was to put a price on the average life. Using questionnaire data (how much extra would a person pay to fly on a safe airline), government statistics on the costs of accident prevention, and personal expenditure on safety devices, the estimated cost ranged from $500 000 to $3 million. Further adjustments are made for life expectancy. In cases of injury rather than death, there is a further mathematical formula for calculating just how much of life's pleasures the victim will forfeit over time.

It is not beyond the realms of possibility to imagine a bank being sued for hedonic damages for failing to make a loan to an individual who claims to have met the bank's lending criteria. Looking at trends in legislation, the burden of proof would rest with the bank rather than the customer. All the more reason for ensuring that in a lending decision the canons of lending are augmented by the canons of ethical banking.

6.7 EDUCATING CUSTOMERS

Perhaps the major challenge for ethical banking is the education of customers in the operations, products and services of a bank. Such training will call for innovative methods to capture the time and attention of busy people. Videos, customer parties, branch open days, customer roundtables and attractive literature all have a part to play in the educational process.

Ethical banking would preclude making extravagant claims for a bank's service. Customers must not feel they are being brainwashed, but that they are being helped to benefit more fully from the products and services of their bank.

6.8 PUBLISHING CHARGES

The need to publish and justify charges will be made easier if customers perceive that they are getting value for money. This will depend on:

— what is offered by the competition;
— the extent to which customers perceive that they are receiving an ethical service;
— the added-value content of products arising from quality of service;
— the distinctiveness of the product/service provided;
— the professionalism of staff;
— the quality of premises, literature and other tangibles.

If a bank adopts the canons of ethical banking and avoids the ethical traps, it should find no difficulty in justifying its charges. A key factor is that the manager and staff believe that the charges are justifiable. Where doubt exists in the minds of staff it will be communicated to customers.

6.9 EXPLAINING DECISIONS

Ethical banking will not make it easier to give the reasons to a customer for declining a loan or some other service; it will make it easier to justify them.

Reasons for declining business generally fall into four categories:

(1) Financial, i.e. doubts *re* proposition, ability to repay, security.
(2) Economic, i.e. type of industry, location, competition.
(3) Personal, i.e. track record, character, health.
(4) Ethical, i.e. nature of proposition, bank policy.

Ethical banking encourages openness and trust between banker and customer. There may be sound legal reasons (potential action for slander) for limiting explanations of declining a lending proposal, but where possible full reasons should be given together with how the proposal might be restructured. Naturally, care has to be taken to avoid too much time being taken up in such explanations. If, however, there is an established procedure and simple explanatory documentation this can speed up the process.

Ethical banking would suggest that all customers making a loan application for the first time should be provided with guidelines, not only on preparing the proposal, but also forewarning them of the reasons why it might be declined.

6.10 GATHERING PERSONAL DATA

Technology enables banks to use customer data in many ways. From credit scoring to direct marketing, computers provide opportunities to tap into a comprehensive data basis. Legislation to reduce racial and sex discrimination is likely to curtail the data which banks can demand from customers wishing to open an account or take out a loan.

A bank practising the canons of ethical banking will be in a better position to elicit additional information from customers on a voluntary basis, since it will be trusted to use it sensitively.

Increasing restrictions will be imposed on how a bank can use its data base for direct mailing or for poaching business from competitors. Here again, proactive action which defines the criteria which a bank will apply to using customer data will give it a competitive advantage in gaining voluntary inputs from customers who will have discretion in the amount of data they supply and its subsequent use.

6.11 THE BANKING OMBUDSMAN SCHEME

This scheme was established by a consortium of leading British banks in 1985. It covers bank services provided by all major banks and some other financial institutions. The geographical scope of the scheme encompasses England, Wales, Scotland and Northern Ireland, but not the Channel Islands or the Isle of Man.

The way the scheme operates for a customer with a complaint or grievance is as follows:

Step 1 – Customer should try to sort out problem with his/her local branch.

Step 2 – If not resolved locally, the complaint must be pursued through all the internal complaint processes of the bank.

Step 3 – Should the customer feel that the complaint is being bogged down in the various procedures of the bank, a letter can be written to the Ombudsman. This will simply be noted.

Step 4 – The bank should either resolve the problem or tell the customer that it has reached deadlock.

Step 5 – Only now can the customer bring the Ombudsman into play, and that is providing that the approach is made within six months of reaching deadlock with the bank.

Step 6 – The Ombudsman checks that the complaint is within his jurisdiction and that deadlock has been reached.

Step 7 – Satisfied that there is a case for the bank to answer, the Ombudsman will ask the customer to send him relevant documents, agree to the case being dealt with under the scheme and authorise the bank to release the relevant information.

Step 8 – Usually, the Ombudsman will try to sort out matters informally and encourage both parties to reach agreement.

Step 9 – When the informal approach fails, the Ombudsman will usually seek formal presentations by both parties and then make a recommendation.

Step 10 – The Ombudsman can make an award of up to £100 000 if he feels the customer is right. Customers do not have to accept his decision but can pursue their case through the courts if they wish.

The scheme, which is free, is available to individuals or groups such as partnerships and clubs, but not companies.

The Ombudsman can deal with a wide range of complaints arising from the many types of services provided through bank branches. He also deals with complaints about credit cards, some bank executor and trustee services, as well as bank services relating to taxation and insurance.

6.12 THE OMBUDSMAN AND ETHICAL BANKING

The Ombudsman scheme is one of last resort. The initiative for invoking it rests with the customer. In that respect it could be argued that the scheme does not comply with the second canon of ethical banking – fairly balanced in the interests of both parties.

There are ten types of complaints which the Ombudsman cannot handle:

(1) The customer's complaint is not against a member of the scheme

(2) The complaint is being or has been dealt with by a court or similar body. (Banks can, if they wish, waive this restriction.)
(3) The complaint comes within the scope of other complaints procedures, set in train by the Financial Services Act 1986, to deal with investment matters.
(4) The complaint relates to a bank's *commercial* judgement in decisions about lending or security.
(5) The complaint relates to a banking service provided on special terms to a customer (or spouse) who is an employee of the bank concerned.
(6) The complaint is about the manner in which a bank has exercised its discretion under a will or trust, or about any lack of consultation in exercising that discretion.
(7) The complaint concerns a bank's general interest rate policies or *other general policy matters*.
(8) The complaint concerns a guarantee or charge given to a bank to support a company.
(9) The complaint concerns banking services provided abroad.
(10) The complaint is a claim for more than £100 000 (or is part of a claim for more than that amount).

It will be seen from the above list that the vast majority of matters which raise issues of morality have to be resolved within a bank and, principally at local level, by ethical banking.

6.13 LAWS AGAINST FRAUD

With the rise in international crime it has been necessary to introduce laws to control what might be called 'unethical customers' – unfortunately, a gross understatement when it comes to drug traffickers and terrorist groups. The most important of these acts in terms of ethical banking are:

(a) The Drug Trafficking Offences Act 1986 allows seizure of a suspect's assets including bank accounts.
(b) The Financial Services Act 1986 regulates the sale of securities and financial products.
(c) The Insolvency Act 1986 provides tough penalties for unethical or even incompetent company directors.

(d) The Banking Act 1987 imposes obligations of disclosures on banks in fraud and other criminal cases.
(e) The Criminal Justice Act 1987 established the Serious Fraud Office and (in 1988) made insider dealing an extraditable offence with a penalty of up to seven years' imprisonment.

These Acts, in the main, strengthen the canons of fairness, social legitimacy and justification. However, they weaken the canon of confidentiality principally for criminals, but it can pose a threat to ethical customers. Interpreting these laws in day-to-day situations can prove a minefield for bankers.

6.14 CONCLUSION

In this chapter we have considered the impact of impending legislation on banker–customer relationships. Drawing on the Report of the Review Committee on Banking Services Law, a possible code would provide a solid foundation for those aspects of ethical banking which are concerned with:

— Fairness and transparency in the banker–customer relationship.
— Confidence in the security of the banking system.
— A bank's duty of confidentiality to its customer.

The trends in current bank legislation and consumer legislation which affect banking are:

(1) A bias towards customers' rights and bankers' duties.
(2) Burden of proof in disputes rests with banks.
(3) Customer education will become a responsibility of banks.
(4) Details of charges will be made public.
(5) Decisions to decline loans will need to be explained to customers.
(6) There will be greater limits in the banks' ability to gather and use customer data.

The implications of these trends for ethical banking was seen to be positive. Those banks which take the initiative to implant the canons of ethical banking before being enforced to abide by evolving legislation will gain a competitive advantage.

7 Ethical Banking – the Cutting Edge of Service Quality

7.1 INTRODUCTION

The 1980s witnessed a new phenomenon in service industries – the existence of customers. Banks have invested millions in 'customer care', 'service quality' programmes with varying degrees of success. I have been deeply involved in the design and implementation of such programmes for ten years. My experience in Britain, Ireland and the United States has shown that certain preconditions are necessary for ethical banking to take root (see Table 7.1).

Ethical banking with its emphasis on the importance of values in interacting with the customer is at the cutting edge of service quality. In the 1990s, service quality will be the field of play for competition between banks and ethical banking will provide the essential weapon for success.

7.2 NEW HORIZONS IN SERVICE QUALITY

Service quality is a never ending journey. This chapter suggests the new horizons banks should be striding towards if they are to sustain a service quality differentiation. Some horizons will be more distant than others, but all of them need to be kept in focus.

The new horizons are:

(a) Using technology to enhance service quality;
(b) Nurturing the customer to reap the full benefits of service quality;
(c) Measuring the financial benefits of service quality;
(d) Reinforcing a freedom-to-serve culture;
(e) Mastering the psychic aspects of banking;
(f) Providing different levels of service.

Each horizon has implications for ethical banking.

Table 7.1   Preconditions for ethical banking

STRATEGIC

Agreed and defined ethical values
Clearly defined mission statement
Customer focused business plans
Understanding of ethical banking
Ethically based personnel and training policies
Ethically based products and procedures
Top level commitment to the canons of ethical banking

SYSTEMS

Clearly defined ethical standards and practices
Customer focused transmission and delivery systems
Clearly defined accountabilities
Effective channels of communication
Tolerance for flexibility
Support systems and other mechanisms for:
— Identifying customer needs and expectations
— Meeting the needs in a manner which exceeds expectations
— Monitoring competitor activity
— Monitoring and anticipating financial and business trends
Competitive service quality standards
A portfolio of measures for the standards
Audit systems which incorporate ethical and quality matters
Procedures for eliciting comments and suggestions from staff and customers
Means for determining costs of ethically based initiatives
Means for determining costs of non-compliance with ethical standards

STAFF

Stimulation of ethical awareness
Training in all aspects of ethical banking
Encouragement of a customer-focused approach
Knowledge of ethical banking and their role in it
Performance appraisal which reinforces ethical behaviour
Sound communications
Fostering of openness and trust
Empowerment of individuals to contribute to the best of their ability
Team building
Encouragement to keep close to the customer
Sustaining a spirit of ethical banking despite hitches
Willingness to share ideas and experiences for the benefit of the customer,
   both internally and in the market-place

7.3 SERVICE TECHNOLOGY

It has long been recognised in banks that technology can vastly improve service delivery. Looking ahead the major service quality issues to be addressed are:

- Use of expert systems (artificial intelligence) to increase responsiveness, reduce risk and provide greater consistency in decision-taking. The service quality challenge is to avoid an impersonal relationship with the customer and a sense of 'redundancy' in bank officials.

- Reinforcing ethical banking by using technology in relation to:
    Comprehensive customer profile information systems;
    Integrated account statements;
    Technology based 'core' services, e.g. financial planning systems.
  The service quality challenge is to use the technology as a basis for differentiating service levels while allowing access to its benefits by any customer willing to pay for a specific technological service.

- Continuing to meet mass marketing banking needs through:
    Electronic delivery systems;
    Counter based automation;
    Automated systems for opening accounts and providing loans.
  The service quality challenge is to reconcile economies of scale by sharing facilities with competitors, yet maintain a competitive advantage.

With the advance of technology there will be a change in the role of branch staff. The skills of selling, persuading and counselling will outweigh those of decision-taking, risk assessment and financial judgement. Branches will become the base from which officials will visit customers rather than the 'office' at which customers meet officials. Staff will need to be sensitive to ethical issues arising from this new mobility. For example, they may accidentally be made privy to personal details of a customer's situation which the customer did not wish to disclose.

As the speed of technological change accelerates, it will no longer provide a competitive advantage *per se*. That will be determined by the manner in which technology is blended with the human element to provide a distinctive tone of service quality.

7.4 NURTURING THE CUSTOMER

While it might be exaggerating to say that traditionally banks have profited from the ignorance of customers, there is no doubt that customers are becoming more demanding. As we have seen, advertising, the mass media and consumer activists have raised levels of expectations and this trend will continue. Unfortunately, this can create unrealistic expectations which result in a negative view of banks. The deliberate creation of false expectations is unethical.

A strategy for nurturing customers will become increasingly important because:

— Customers tend to close their accounts because of dissatisfaction with the poor service quality they have received rather than their experience of good service quality with the competitor to whom they move their accounts.
— Market research shows that the more knowledgeable customers are about how banks operate, the more confident they feel and the more open they are to cross-selling.
— Legislation from 1992 onwards will give rise to high legal costs in defending even unjustified claims against banks.
— An increasing proportion of earnings will come from commissions and fees. For this to succeed, customers must be convinced that they are receiving value for money.

Educating customers is not new, but has tended to be carried out on a hit or miss basis by leaving around brochures or giving written instructions on documents. The new horizons in educating customers will be marked by:

(a) A strategy geared to each service quality customer segment.
(b) The use of video and interactive techniques for teaching customers.
(c) Advertising geared to educating rather than promoting or 'knocking'.
(d) The provision of different types of 'financial clinics' by banks rather than voluntary organisations, e.g. debt counselling.

The ethical challenge will be to market the customer education process so that customers are motivated to learn in a way which will lead to higher profits for the bank.

7.5 MEASURING FINANCIAL BENEFITS

Service quality is a profit strategy. In broad terms, profitability is a function concerned with maximising margins and minimising costs. It is usually difficult in financial services to identify the profit contribution of service quality (or any other discrete factor). On the other hand, it is usually possible to identify the costs of providing different levels of service.

The concept of service quality sensitises an organisation to the costs of defective service. It has been calculated in various research studies that up to 30 per cent of staff time is devoted to rectifying mistakes. There are two areas of cost to be considered – direct costs and 'ripple' costs. The latter are those which ripple through an organisation even after a mistake is rectified.

The service quality challenge is to:

- Isolate income which comes from:
    Service charges accepted by the mass market;
    Premiums paid for specific services;
    Direct cost savings accruing from service quality initiatives;
    Ripple cost savings.

This cost consciousness must be kept in harness with service consciousness. The aim of service quality is not to reduce costs but to induce customers to pay willingly for the service which they receive. Achieving this aim will call in many instances for ethical decision-making on how best to balance profitability and customer satisfaction.

7.6 REINFORCING A FREEDOM-TO-SERVE CULTURE

In recent years, 'freedom-to-manage' is a shibboleth which has sounded throughout banks; it is symptomatic of a culture of stewardship born of the fiduciary responsibilities of banking. Times are changing; banks can boost their own products and provide an ever increasing range of them. Freedom-to-manage will not necessarily result in a service culture. Such a culture calls for freedom-to-serve.

Freedom-to-serve does not mean anarchy or satisfying the whim of every customer regardless of costs. Rather, it is the acceptance across the organisation that doing what is right to satisfy a customer has precedence over other activities. It involves devising policies, procedures and systems which are customer oriented and encourages giving the customer the benefit of the doubt.

This is no easy task in banking. It calls for a specifying of service standards and measures to avoid errors; a building of mutual trust to reduce suspicion; an acceptance of mutual dependence by staff and customer; a recognition that mistakes will be made but should be used as learning opportunities rather than reasons for punishment. Above all, it calls for compliance with the canons of ethical banking.

A freedom-to-serve culture makes heavy demands on management at all levels in the organisation. It needs careful management development supported by a raft of sound service delivery systems and clearly defined ethical values.

7.7 MASTERING THE PSYCHIC ASPECTS OF BANKING

As technology covers more of the financial aspects of banking, the role of the banker will focus increasingly on the psychic aspects. The challenge will be to convey to customers that the banker is on the same wavelength as themselves.

In Chapter 4 mention was made of the aureole effect, whereby the perspective of the customer in a given situation often encompasses a wider vision than that perceived by the banker. The importance of recognising this concept in dealing with customers cannot be overstressed. Mastery lies in identifying the psychic aspects of customer relationships. Examples are shown in Table 7.2.

All banker–customer relationships take place within a 'service encounter'. Every day customers are involved in service encounters – interacting with providers of service. Whether it be cashing a cheque, ordering a meal, buying a newspaper, arranging a funeral, every encounter we have with an organisation results in an evaluation of its service quality.

A service encounter need not involve face-to-face contact: letters, telephone calls or using cash dispensers are just as much service encounters as being served by an individual. The way in which each encounter is managed plays a major part in a customer's perception of service quality.

Much customer service training has concentrated on developing people skills of those who come into contact with the public. Smiling, eye-contact, listening, all have their part to play in providing cus-

Table 7.2 Opportunities for new thinking on psychic aspects of ethical banking

Arena	Psychic Aspects
	(Thought provokers – not intended to be exhaustive nor definitive)
Market Segmentation	Responding to needs of: Service minimalists Service sensitives Service premium payers Tuning into 'mind states' Borrower mind states Investor mind states Saver mind states
Product Development	Psychic value-added opportunities Life changes Marriage Separation University First job Redundancy Retirement Bereavement Life surprises (bad) Serious accident Serious illness Permanent disability Business collapse Bankruptcy Sudden death Life surprises (good) Big lottery win Big prize bond win Inheritance Award of large legal damages
Delivery Systems	Personal security and self-service Understanding of 'technology' Bolstering self-esteem through self-service Self-service for old/disabled Minimising hassle
Information Technology	Comfort levels for techno-phobes

(continued on page 102)

Table 7.2 continued

Arena	Psychic Aspects
Information Technology (cont.)	Recovery systems for 'breakdowns' Raising tolerance levels for: 'out of service' Faults New systems Raising skill levels for self-service
Service Ergonomics	Clarity/location/impact of signage Counter/desk levels Ease of use of: Equipment Writing materials Design of documents Design of: Cheque books Lodgement books Statements Ease of opening envelopes by old/ disabled (security considerations)
Corporate Identity	Influencing mind-sets *re* banks, big organisations, national characteristics Conveying distinctive 'style' Managing 'bad news'

tomer satisfaction. Nevertheless, much training fails to stick because insufficient attention is paid to the way in which the experience of the customer can be managed in any service encounter. Two factors influence customer satisfaction in an encounter:

(1) Context
(2) Pacing

7.7.1 Context

Every encounter is part of the chain of service in which the customer is involved. There are three types of encounter in which a customer finds him/herself at any point in time:

(a) Transforming encounters

(b) Facilitating encounters

(c) Chores

Transforming encounters take place in a context of life-changing situations for the customer. Facilitating encounters take place in a context of life-enhancing situations for the customer. Chores are in the context of 'forced need' situations – they involve the customer in doing something which he/she would prefer to avoid or which in itself gives little satisfaction.

Transforming Encounters

These are the least frequent types of encounter. They range from those associated with major life events – birth, marriage, death – to other significant situations. Buying a house, setting up a business, undergoing major surgery, are all transforming encounters.

Whatever the type of transformation, a core of common features comes into play and needs to be managed by the service provider:

- Anxiety – 'Am I doing the right thing?'
- Suspicion – 'Am I getting the best advice/treatment?'
- Dependency – 'Just tell me what to do and I'll do it if it means all will be well.'
- Vulnerability – 'What happens if things go wrong?'

Facilitating Encounters

Holidays, anniversary celebrations, buying a new car, getting the loan you want, are examples of life-enhancing situations. They do not change lives but they give it a little more zest than would otherwise be the case. Such encounters are eagerly awaited – the dream holiday, the dream car, the dream dress. All the worse, therefore, when the dream does not materialise or is spoiled in some way. When expectations are not met service quality is perceived at best as mediocre.

Managing facilitating encounters calls for careful attention to a different set of factors from those found in transforming encounters:

- Idealised expectations – 'It's not like it is in the adverts.'
- Swift gratification – 'I want it now.'
- Security of self-esteem – 'I *can* understand the menu, thank you.'
- Low tolerance for mishaps – 'I want everything to go smoothly.'

The service provider must be able to manage facilitating encounters by:

- Managing expectations – 'You may find the plumbing in Mongolia rather primitive.'
- Swift responsiveness – 'We'll get it to you quicker than anyone else.'
- Reinforcing self-esteem – 'Most people find this a problem, so do you mind if I just go over the main points?'
- Swift compensation – 'Sorry for that mishap; please have a drink on the house.'
- Flexibility – 'We'll cope with that change of plans straight away.'

Chores

This type of encounter is the most common. A chore is a recurrent routine or tedious task; although we tend to place emphasis on the tedious aspect, it is used here in its wider meaning. The weekly shopping, paying bills, cashing cheques, travelling in the rush hour, returning faulty goods, chasing up unfulfilled promises are all chores.

Managing this type of encounter in a manner which makes the chore more bearable calls for recognition of the following characteristics displayed by customers involved in chores:

- Boredom – 'I'm tired of doing this week after week.'
- Aggression – 'You had better sort this out – I'm sick of chasing you.'
- Exaggeration – 'I've phoned you a hundred times about this.'
- Special pleading – 'I don't care if it is acceptable to others, what *I* want is . . .'
- Disenchantment – 'You're all the same when it comes to . . .'

Chores generally are not enjoyable occasions for either the service provider or the customer, but they can be made more tolerable by:

- Diversion – reducing boredom by use of background music, video displays, newspapers, cups of coffee.
- Empathy – 'I know this must be a nuisance. We'll deal with this right away.'
- Rational responding – 'I know it must seem a long time to you but in fact it has only been . . .'

- Anticipating – Having clearly defined standards and practices for handling complaints.
- Forewarning – 'I thought you had better know that because of X we will not be able to meet the deadline.'
- Apologising – 'I'm sorry you have had to go to such trouble.'
- Cheerfulness – Smiling, eye-contact, greeting.

Other ways of reducing the negative aspects of chores include:

- Partial self-service, such as at petrol stations, supermarkets.
- Full self-service, such as cash dispensers, vending machines.
- Competitions.
- Stimulating decor.

Having identified the context within which the customer is operating, the ethical banker has to pace the customer in order to establish rapport.

7.7.2 Pacing

Contacts with customers are likely to more effective if we remember that:

(a) Our behaviour will influence the customer's behaviour – and vice versa if we so choose;
(b) We can each choose the type of behaviour we show to the customer;
(c) The type of behaviour which we choose will either help or hinder us in complying with the canons of ethical banking.

A key factor in pacing a customer is to be able to establish quick rapport by getting on the same wavelength in terms of both product needs and psychic needs.

The reason for emphasising the psychic aspect of face-to-face contact is that when emotions run high, dealing with the product needs of a customer ought to be preceded by responding to the emotional needs. What the banker may recognise as an administrative error will be perceived by the customer as a source of embarassment, hurt or injured self-esteem.

We can convey a sense of care even when we cannot fully satisfy the customer's product needs. There are several techniques which staff can be encouraged to practise:

(1) Listening carefully to what the customer is saying and regularly checking that each understands the other.
(2) Finding our similar likes or dislikes and strengthening rapport by spending a little time on these.
(3) Talking at a similar speed to that which the customer uses.
(4) Observing body language for signs of impatience, anxiety, confusion; these signs can more accurately reflect what the customer is *feeling* than do words.
(5) Using a tone of voice which is soothing and/or neutral, no matter how provoked (within the bounds of normal civilised behaviour).
(6) Where possible using patterns of speech similar to that of the customer. Many people tend to use a particular pattern more than others.

Patterns of Speech

Our patterns of speech tend to relate to one or more of the five senses:

Sight
Hearing
Touch and movement
Smell
Taste

When using a pattern based on *sight* people want you to *focus* so that you can *see* things from their *point of view*. They want you to share the same *perspective* so that you can *observe* their *bright* ideas. This will lead to a shared *overview* with both of you agreeing that *seeing* is believing.

At other times, customers may be using a speech pattern based on *hearing*. They will ask you to *listen* to what they are *telling* you. They may claim that they *hear* what you are getting at but that it does not *sound* right. Discussion will continue until you *strike a chord* by saying something that *rings true*; then they will be *all ears*.

Less common is a speech pattern based on touch and movement types of words. Those using this pattern may *soothe* you or *rub* you up the wrong way, depending on where you *stand* on an issue. When you *grasp* what you *hold* to be true, they *feel* happy. But you may not want to *follow* their *stance*. Do not let them *walk all over you*; faced with the same *position*, they would not *take* things *lying down*. Ideas *hit* them and they have *gut feelings*. They hope that you will keep in *touch*.

Generally, the least common pattern relates to smell and taste; these are usually linked by people in their conversation. Such people talk of *sniffing out* opportunities, or giving a *taste* of their own medicine. When business is bad it *stinks* – possibly because of *rotten* luck – which, of course, they find *distasteful*.

While not wishing to exaggerate the importance of speech patterning, it has been found to be a useful tool in establishing and maintaining rapport. Two people talking on the *same* subject, but using (usually unconsciously) different speech patterns, are likely to have greater difficulty in communicating than will those using the same pattern.

Naturally, patterns change between people and even the same person may use different patterns at different times. The trick is to encourage staff to identify the pattern that the customer is using and to respond to it on the same basis.

For example:

CUSTOMER: I really don't see what you are getting at.
BANKER: Let me put it in a clearer perspective. Look at it this way.

CUSTOMER: This doesn't sound right to me.
BANKER: I hear what you're saying. Let's see if this strikes a chord.

CUSTOMER: I'm sorry, but I just can't grasp all you are saying.
BANKER: Let us move more slowly then. We'll take each point step by step. When you feel that you've got a hold on a point we'll pass on to the next step.

CUSTOMER: I'm afraid I smell a rat in these proposals.
BANKER: Let's see if we can make things more palatable. Once we've cleared the air I think you'll find everything more to your taste.

Table 7.3 provides guidance on how to adopt an ethical approach to dealing with customers in different types of situations. The essence of ethical banking is not to take advantage of distress, but to work in partnership with the customer in finding a mutually acceptable solution.

Table 7.3 Ethical techniques for dealing with customers

State of mind of customer	Behavioural indicators	Possible causes	Techniques for counteracting
Anger – a state of extreme displeasure	Choice of language tends to aggressiveness Loudness of language Quick breathing Not permitting interruptions Piling complaint on complaint ('and another thing') *Visual* Penetrating stare causing the lids to tense Brows lowered and drawn together Lips pressed together or opened and pushed forward	Promise not kept Mistake in procedure Behaviour of bank employees Prolonged waiting Personal circumstances	Recognise that anger though directed at you is caused by a situation which needs to be 'put right' in customer's perception Listen for clues as to cause of anger Remain calm Convey sympathy with neutral phrases e.g. 'I see'; 'I understand'; 'You must be upset' Reduce the emotional level by promising to enquire and to phone back within an agreed time-frame If customer is abusive say firmly that you want to help but that it is in both parties interest that you terminate the call and will call back If you feel yourself getting angry, hang up politely and promise to call back

Critical – a state of fault-finding	*Oral* Tone (cool or aggressive) Choice of words Impersonal approach *Visual* Momentary closing of eyes Raising of shoulders	Expectations not met Promises not met Mistake in procedure Ignorance of procedure Misunderstanding	Do not interrupt Apologise even if criticism unjustified ('I'm sorry you felt you had to ring us') Promise and specify speedy action if criticism justified Offer specific or general help ('Is there anything we can do in the meantime?') Thank customer for bringing matter to your notice Summarise the main action to be taken
Frustration – a state of discontentment through inability to achieve one's desires	*Oral* Choice of language Tone (pleading or aggressive) Emphasis on time-spans/deadlines Eagerness to establish rapport with service provider *Visual* Finger tapping Eyes looking upwards	Unrealistic expectations Fault in procedures Unkept promises Time pressures Being passed from department to department	Listen Indicate sympathy Empathise – 'It must have been annoying' Commit yourself to doing something – even if it is only phoning back Explore alternative ways of removing/reducing the frustration level – 'Would it help if we . . .?'

(continued on page 110)

Table 7.3 continued

State of mind of customer	Behavioural indicators	Possible causes	Techniques for counteracting
Ignorance – a state of lacking knowledge and understanding of a subject	*Oral* Choice of language Tone (subservient or aggressive) Expressions of low self-esteem Lots of questions Pauses after receiving answers *Visual* Fidgeting Looking downwards	Lack of familiarity with financial matters Unable to understand jargon Physical disability hearing/sight Low literacy	Put at ease Reassure customer that their ignorance is common. ('Most people have problems with that') Give concise answers and check understanding frequently ('To check that I have explained things properly; would you please summarise the main points as you understand them?')
Remorse – a state of bitter regret for a wrong doing or mistake	*Oral* Choice of language Tone Emphasis on personal feelings Confessional approach ('I need to get this off my chest') Quieter voice than normal *Visual* Avoiding eye contact Wringing of hands	Overcommitted financially Has wrong type of loan for current needs Failure to admit ignorance Previous bad behaviour now seen to be unjustified	Listen Put at ease Use 'para-linguistics' to indicate your interest e.g. 'Uhms'; 'Ohs'; 'Ahs' Reduce guilt feelings by reassuring that this is not a unique situation Suggest ways of reducing guilt and maintaining self-esteem ('Why not reduce your payments and then increase them when things get better?')

	Oral / Visual	Causes	Response
			Offer alternative courses of action wherever possible Maintain regular contact to make customer feel wanted and correct in original decision
Worry – a state of lacking peace of mind *Note:* This is a very broad category, but it is included to cover undefined concerns of customers	*Oral* Choice of language Tone Chattering Lack of listening *Visual* Foot jabbing Staring at some object Clasping of hands	Personal problems Stress Insecurity Ill health Financial problems	Listen Convey sense of professionalism and stewardship Seek to identify core cause of worry without appearing to pry Convey sympathy Highlight alternative courses of action Promise a follow-up call, 'to see how things are going' Show caring by offering to perform a small task which means a lot to the customer. 'Don't worry; I'll phone *X* and ask them to get in touch with you'
Grief – a state of deep sorrow	*Oral* Choice of language Tone (subdued) Long pauses Crying	Death Serious illness Separation or other unpleasant life-change	Listen Do not rush conversation Accept longer than usual pauses before seeking an answer Convey sympathy in an unforced

(continued on page 112)

112

Table 7.3 continued

State of mind of customer	Behavioural indicators	Possible causes	Techniques for counteracting
	'Swallowing' words Deep breathing *Visual* Weeping Wringing of hands Distant look		manner Empathise – 'I know how you must be feeling' Display sensitive firmness when required. 'I fully understand that this is a difficult time to be asking these questions but unless we have the answers we cannot . . .'. Give option to deal with situation in several stages ('if you prefer we can leave it for the moment and talk some more tomorrow – what would be a convenient time for me to phone?')

Figure 7.1   Service quality level planning grid

Product/Market Segments: Commercial ───────→

	Self-employed	Small business	Large business	International
Premium				
Superior				
Enhanced				
Standard				

Service quality levels

Guidance on completing the Service Quality Level Planning Grid

1. Define the product/market segments relevant to your branch.
2. Identify key customers in each product/market segment and the level of service quality which the record shows will meet their requirements.
3. Position customers in each segment.

Note: Planning grids should also be devised for personal, agricultural and other sectors.

7.8   PROVIDING DIFFERENT LEVELS OF SERVICE

Although ethical standards must be applied in a uniform manner to all customers, service standards can vary. In fact a consequence of ethical banking will be to acknowledge that service levels will vary, dependent on the amount a customer is willing to pay for the service.

Figure 7.1 shows a service quality level planning grid which can help the ethical banker to segment customers on the basis of service provided. The example is for the business sector. Table 7.4 itemises the possible factors which can differentiate each service level.

Table 7.4 Service quality levels: possible differentiation factors

Level	Differentiation factors
Standard – meets the needs of customers in a manner which is marginally better than that available from the competition	Behaviour Courtesy Communications Empathy Competence Premises Cleanliness Layout Signage Limited privacy Access During normal opening hours Normally officer grade is highest contact
Enhanced – meets the needs of customers and exceeds their expectations in a number of ways which clearly outmatch the competition	Behaviour As above Premises As above – plus Privacy except for minor matters Access During normal working hours Normally Asst Manager is highest contact level Access to specialists Flexibility Tolerance on small lapses *re* arrangements Provided with limited range of options on saving/borrowing needs
Superior – meets the needs of customers and exceeds their expectations on a broad front in ways that are clearly superior to the competition	Behaviour As above Premises As above – plus Complete privacy when requested

Table 7.4   *continued*

Level	Differentiation factors
Superior (cont.)	Access
	Appointments arranged outside normal hours if required
	Will be seen without appointment
	Will be met at other locations
	Normally the manager or deputy manager is point of contact when requested
	Introduced to specialists at short notice
	Invited to meal or drinks at bank sponsored function once a year.
	Flexibility
	Needs anticipated as far as possible
	Minimal demands for data (assuming current in-bank records available)
	Any contact with several parts of the bank is smoothly coordinated
	Speed of response
	Rapid reaction
	Deadlines met or preceded
	Possible extras
	'Personal banker' overlooking all accounts
	Receives bank publications, bank diary or similar
	Receives 'Can I help you?' telephone call from manager, if

(continued on page 116)

Table 7.4   *continued*

Level	Differentiation factors
Superior (cont.)	appropriate, at least twice per year
Premium – meets the needs and exceeds the expectations of customers in a manner which is consistently of a higher order than that available from the competition	Differentiation factors as for superior service plus Complete privacy at all times Seen at virtually any time by some official File regularly reviewed to identify opportunities to provide improved service quality Regularly invited to bank sponsored prestige events and other special occasions Initialed desk diary or other item Lunch/dinner with an executive at least once per year Car parking arranged when visiting branch Introductions arranged to significant contacts Help provided when overseas by bank or corresponding banks 'Account executive' keeps watchful eye on relationship where more than £ million savings or loan accounts

Ethical banking requires a clear and detailed statement of what a bank provides for customers in terms of reliability, responsiveness, courtesy and so forth. For example, reliability encompasses a multitude of activities ranging from data reliability to professional reliability. Table 7.5 shows how the ethical banker should approach the task of enhancing reliability and speed of service.

Table 7.5 Planning to enhance reliability and speed of service

Key result areas (examples)	Service objective
Data reliability i.e. no mistakes in data provided orally or in writing	To provide our customers with a more reliable quality of service than that available from the competition
Competence reliability i.e. advice on products and procedures will prove dependable	
Systems reliability i.e. equipment of all types operates without breakdown	
Maintenance reliability i.e. all maintenance checks are carried out on a regular basis	
Promise reliability i.e. promises are kept and often exceeded	
Professional reliability i.e. business is conducted in an ethical and lawful manner	

Service quality standards and measures for reliability

Standards set for	Examples of benchmark standards	Measures
Opening times of branches/departments	Open/close within one minute of published time	Spot checks
Closing times of branches/departments		Customer roundtables
Time-keeping of staff	All staff have at least an $x\%$ keeping attendance record	Time-keeping/absence records
	Error rate will be no more than $x\%$ per month	

(continued on page 118)

Service quality standards and measures for reliability

Standards set for	Examples of benchmark standards	Measures
Accuracy in:	No more than x% of documents to be returned to originator for correction prior to issue	Simple sampling, e.g. checking one in ten of any document issued/received
Statements		Service measurement charts
Letters		Maintaining a complaints/compliments log
Telephone messages		Short weekly reviews of branch/department reliability performance
Faxes		Customer questionnaires
Legal documents		
Advertising		
Product support literature		
Circulars		
Customer records		
Loan applications		
Customer/staff names and addresses		
Credit scoring data		
Standing orders		
Direct debit instructions		

Planning to enhance speed of service

Key service quality result areas (examples)	Service quality objective
Speed of response to a request for existing information, e.g. balance of account	To respond to and meet customers' needs more swiftly than competitors
Speed in processing data e.g. transferring money from one account to another	

Speed in dealing with the unusual e.g. quoting exchange rates for uncommon currencies
Speed in decision-taking e.g. granting or declining a loan application
Speed in conveying decision e.g. using fax or telephone in preference to a letter

Standards set for	Possible Standards	Measures
Answering telephones	Calls will be acknowledged by fourth ring	Spot checks Phone branch/office and check time lapses Customer questionnaire
Time lapse for returning calls	No caller left holding for more than x seconds without option of being called or calling again	
Time lapse for acknowledging letters	No more than x% of letters to go unacknowledged within two working days of receipt	End of day count of unacknowledged letters Service measurement chart
Time lapse for answering letters	All letters to be fully answered/further acknowledged within five working days of receipt	End of week count of letters received/acknowledged
Queuing times	Maximum queuing times for different types of service to be defined	Customer questionnaires Service Quality Measurement Chart

(continued on page 120)

Standards set for	Possible Standards	Measures
Speed of acknowledging presence of a customer	Person to be acknowledged within one minute of entering branch	Random observation Application of appropriate service quality practice
Speed of arranging appointments	All appointment requests to be met by an official within a maximum of three working days of request Appointment with a specific official to be arranged within five days	Diary of lapsed time between request and appointment
Speed of correcting errors	$x\%$ of minor errors corrected immediately $x\%$ of significant errors corrected within one day Level of recurring errors reduced by $x\%$ within y months	End of day/week performance review Service quality measurement charts Complaints log Customer roundtables Customer questionnaires

Planning to enhance innovations in service quality

Key service quality result areas (examples)	Service quality objective
Improvements to existing service quality, e.g. reduce queuing by publishing a 'Guide to Queuing' giving details of peaks and troughs in queuing times at the branch	To provide more innovative service quality than that available from competitors at the same price

Introduction of new service, e.g. provide a member of staff as 'baby minder' in the office if required by couple with an appointment to discuss substantial loan or savings options

Repackaging of existing services, e.g. hold a 'Family Night' to outline bank products 'from cradle to rest home'

Key result area	Standards set for	Possible standards	Measures
Service innovation	Social initiatives, e.g. disco for young customers	One social initiative per year which leads to a specified increase in good quality accounts	Increase in good quality accounts for targeted segments
	Business initiatives, e.g. 'confidential briefings' for specific business segments	One business initiative per year which leads to identifiable good quality loans or other business	Increase in good quality loans, etc. for targeted business segments
	Service delivery initiatives, e.g. use of faxes, mail shots, delivery of cheques, etc.	Introduce one new service delivery innovation every six months	Evidence of new initiatives and of positive customer response, e.g. from market research or roundtables

Table 7.6 Ethical service quality practices

Service quality objective	Courtesy practices	Measures
To provide a level of courtesy which is consistently superior to that available from the competition	*Conducting transactions* Greeting Eye contact Smiling Thanking Signifying end of transaction or next step	Customer questionnaires Customer roundtables Observation
	Conducting interviews with Customers Time allocation Punctuality Minimal disturbance Availability of relevant data Indication of intent or next step	Diary Time taken to find file Service measurement chart Customer questionnaire Customer roundtable Frequency of interruptions

123

Visiting customers
Checking acceptability
Explaining purpose
Allocating time
Making visit purposeful
to customer
Punctuality
Indicating follow-up action

Staff relations
Welcoming newcomers
Acknowledging good work
Acknowledging changes in
personal circumstances
where appropriate
Disciplining in private
Allocating time for
'personal chats' on work
matters
Maintaining contact
when person is off sick

Diary
Requests for repeat visits
Number of visits declined
Business resulting from visits
Business lost after visits
Customer questionnaires
Customer roundtables
Service measurement chart

Appraisals
Staff meetings
Staff roundtables

(continued on page 124)

Service quality objective	Communications practices	Measures
To communicate with customers at a level appropriate to their understanding of the subject, in a manner that is perceived as superior to the competition	*Telephone service* Adoption of guidelines Development of own 'best practice'	Spot checks Customer questionnaires Service quality measurement charts Weekly/monthly reviews Complaints log Customer roundtables
	Correspondence Adoption of guidelines Development of own 'best practice' Use of 'Child's Guide' where necessary to supplement 'official' document Regular review of content, clarity and tone of all letters – especially those containing 'bad news' Have range of standard letters for marriages, births, deaths, etc.	
	Face to face Adopt courtesy and empathy practices Regularly check understanding by the customer Pace speed of speech to needs of the customer Use language appropriate to the needs of the customer End by checking that customer understands the position to date and the next step	

Service quality objective	Empathy practices	Measures
To convey to all customers a sense of receiving 'the personal touch' in those situations where this would be deemed necessary by the customer; to convey this feeling of empathy in a manner superior to that of the competition	Assess the type of service encounter which the customer perceives as taking place: Transforming encounter (i.e. outcome will have a significant effect on customer) Facilitating encounter (i.e. outcome will make life easier for the customer) Chore encounter (i.e. outcome will either put things right or have neutral/negative effect on the customer) Swift encounter (i.e. relatively trivial needs of the customer will be satisfied swiftly)	Customer questionnaire Customer roundtables Extent to which service encounter objectives of customer/bank are met Service quality measurement chart Complaints/compliments log
	Adjust preparation time, location and pacing to service encounter	Diary
	Provide regular indicators of understanding how customer *feels* Apply courtesy and communications practices	Observation

Finally, ethical banking calls for the adoption of day-to-day behaviour which conforms to specified standards. Table 7.6 gives examples of how this can be specified in terms of courtesy, communications and empathy. The key factor is not to manipulate customers but genuinely to serve them.

7.9   CONCLUSION

Ethical banking is service quality at its best. The customer is perceived not simply as a source of profit, but as an individual whose values have to be taken into account when seeking to satisfy needs and expectations.

New horizons beckon in terms of technology, values, service levels. The psychic side of banking is moving fast; in its wake, ethical issues are coming to the surface and must be confronted.

Ethical banking is not a fad but a natural progression in the evolution of one of the oldest professions in the world. Bankers have made is possible for man to realise his potential sooner than would otherwise have been possible; it has helped dreams to come true; it has enabled peoples to survive. There is a dark side to banking, just as there is a dark side to every human institution. Ethical banking will reduce that black side and provide a financial service better, perhaps than we deserve.

8 Developing Ethical Bankers

8.1 INTRODUCTION

Ethical banking is no accident. It is the outcome of clearly defined policies, moral leadership, sound training practices, regular reinforcement of ethical decision-making and behaviour.

Although the canons of ethical banking have a general relevance, their specific adoption and application will depend on the particular culture and management practices of each bank.

Ethical banking needs to be integrated into the totality of banking operations. Ideally, it should not be separated from other activities. Unfortunately, we do not live in an ideal world; sound ethical standards, decision-making and behaviour cannot be taken for granted. If ethical behaviour was something that happened 'automatically' in banking there would be no need for auditors or inspectors.

It is therefore necessary to establish clear guidelines for ethical policies and practices, codes of conduct and training in ethical decision-taking and behaviour.

8.2 ETHICAL BANKING GUIDELINES

The following are prototypes which a bank can adapt to its particular needs and customs.

8.2.1 Management Responsibility for Company Ethics

Ethics Policy The responsibility for and commitment to ethical banking is vested in the highest level of management. Management must take the necessary action to ensure that ethical banking is defined, understood, actioned and sustained.

Objectives Management must define objectives pertaining to the key elements of ethical banking against the following criteria:

127

(a) The identification and evaluation of conformity with legal requirements of the states in which the bank operates.
(b) The identification and evaluation of conformity with the regulations and requirements of all associations in which the bank participates.
(c) The provision of adequate training and resources to meet legal and quasi-legal requirements and to facilitate ethical banking.
(d) The systematic monitoring of behaviour throughout the bank to ensure that there is full conformity with the canons of ethical banking.
(e) The regular review of problem cases to ensure that they are resolved in accordance with the canons of ethical banking.
(f) The continued assessment of ethical banking relative to evolving customer needs and expectations.
(g) The use of new technology to reinforce ethical standards and measure conformity with them.
(h) The creation of a collective will of ethical behaviour through moral leadership, encouragement and education.

8.2.2 The Ethical Banking System

This consists of the organisational relationships, responsibilities and procedures for safeguarding the integrity of ethical banking. The following aspects are essential to the success of ethical banking:

(1) An ethical banking committee comprising both executive and non-executive directors under the chairmanship of an independent person is appointed by the board to advise on policy, monitor activities, consider cases brought to its attention by:
    Customers
    Employees
    Shareholders
    Suppliers
    Regulatory bodies
    The Board
(2) The ethical banking committee will liaise with the 'audit committee' in situations mutually agreed by both bodies.
(3) Personal integrity in respect of all individuals responsible for making ethical banking a reality. This involves the creation of close cooperation and trust between employees of the bank and customers.
(4) Pursuit by management of the total elimination of unethical

practices as the only viable standard for ethical banking.
(5) Establishing appropriate measures for verification of ethical practices.
(6) Codes of conduct and appropriate procedures defining ethical practices and how they will be monitored.

General and specific accountabilities for complying with ethical standards should be explicitly defined. Clear lines of authority should be established to sustain ethical behaviour. Provision should be made for ensuring that all employees receive appropriate motivation, education and acknowledgement on relevant aspects of ethical banking.

Ethical banking reviews should be conducted annually to determine the continuing suitability of existing ethical standards and measures. Such reviews should include:

— Findings of audits/inspectors' reports.
— Findings of external reviews by regulatory bodies.
— Considerations for updating current ethical banking practices in relation to changes brought about by new technology, mergers and acquisitions, market strategies and social conditions.

Ethical aspects of new products/services should be considered by the management concerned prior to the launch of any new product or service. Areas of ambiguity or doubt should be resolved prior to the launch.

Corrective action for non-compliance with ethical standards should be clearly defined and communicated to employees. Action on non-compliance should be integrated with existing disciplinary procedures wherever possible. Employees who wish to raise concerns on ethical matters arising from the behaviour of colleagues, superiors or the bank as a corporate entity, should be able to seek direct access to a member of the ethical banking committee. In all such cases confidentiality must be respected by both parties. Where a concern or complaint raised by an employee is found by the ethical banking committee to be justified, the employee should be given complete assurance that they will not be disadvantaged in any way by having raised the issue. In the event that the employee feels that such an assurance is not being adhered to he/she should have the right to request a hearing by the ethical banking committee or another party mutually acceptable to both the bank and the employee.

8.3 CODES OF CONDUCT

Wherever possible ethical codes should be drawn up in consultation with representatives of employees so that there is a sense of ownership and reality. The following example is adapted from the code issued by the Bank of Ireland.

Introduction by Chief Executive

The board has given consideration to policy guidelines on ethical banking and deems it appropriate to issue the following statement to all employees of the group:

> The Bank and its subsidiary companies are engaged in the provision of a wide range of financial services in various markets in Ireland and throughout the world. Wherever we operate, we must all ensure that our business is conducted in a manner which is consistent with the longstanding reputation of the Group for the maintenance of the highest standards of integrity in all our business dealings.
>
> As an aid to achieving this objective, the following general principles are laid down:
>
> 1. In all markets in which we operate we are committed to complying in full with the legal, regulatory and other requirements of the jurisdiction concerned.
> 2. All Employees of the Group will act with integrity in all dealings with customers and other parties with whom the Group is connected, and in all internal matters. No Employee should act in a manner which, were such to become a matter of public record, could lead to any injury to our reputation.
>
> Each Employee of the Group has the personal responsibility of compliance with this policy, and since the matter is of such fundamental importance to the Group, any interpretation of its requirements should have regard for both the letter and the spirit thereof.
>
> Where any Employee has, at any time, doubts or concerns about any matter which arises which may relate to compliance with this

policy, he or she should discuss the matter fully with his or her Manager or Head of Department.

[It will be seen that the general principles are in full accord with the canons of legality, fairness, social legitimacy and justification.]

GUIDELINES ON CODE OF CONDUCT

To assist in the achievement of compliance with Group policy in this area, the general guidelines set out below will apply. In addition to these, Executive Management will issue, where required, local guidance, in writing, on any other matters which may arise affecting the work in which particular Group Employees are engaged.

1 Insider Dealing

No Employee of the Group may deal, or advise anyone else to deal, in the stocks or shares of a company that has a business relationship with the Group while in the possession of information of a nature which might impact on the market price of the stock if this information were in the public domain, where such information has come as a result of the relationship with the Group, or in the course of Group business.

In addition, no Employee should, for personal gain or for the benefit of a third party, make use of, or disclose, confidential information learned as a result of employment in the Group.

2 Dealing in Bank Stock

Under normal circumstances, Group Employees may deal freely in Bank Stock only during defined 'window periods' which occur during the course of each year. Dealing includes all purchases and sales of Bank Stock, including such transactions as sale and immediate repurchase (e.g. to crystalise capital gains). These window periods immediately follow the announcement of interim and final Group results, when it is unlikely that Employees in general will possess any price sensitive information concerning Bank Stock. At present, the window periods are defined to be:

— The three weeks following the publication of the interim results.
— The period starting with the announcement of the preliminary results for the year and ending two weeks after the Annual General Court.

Outside the above periods, Employees wishing to deal in Bank Stock must first secure the clearance of their Line Executive for each specific transaction. Executives will confirm each such approval given, in writing, and will retain a copy on record.

Employees of the Group may never deal in Bank of Ireland Stock, either in their own name or through any other party or nominee, or give advice or recommendations on Bank Stock, while in the possession of information of a nature which might impact on the market price of our stock, were such information available in the public domain. This prohibition applies both during and outside the window periods.

3 Conflicts of Interest

(i) Outside Interests

Group Employees are encouraged to participate actively in the communities in which they live and work. The Group is supportive of Employees who undertake for, or accept positions in organisations in their communities which are generally perceived to be non-controversial and of benefit to the community in general, or to sectors thereof, without adversely affecting other sectors.

[Membership of political parties is covered under point 6 of these guidelines.]

However, in normal circumstances, no Employee should hold a position or have an outside interest that materially interferes with the time or attention which should be devoted to his or her work in the Group. Where such an interest, or position, would involve a non-trivial time commitment during normal business hours, the approval of the Employee's Manager must be obtained before-hand.

Involvement in a business of any kind is regarded differently because of the conflicts of interest and other pressures which can develop, the risks of overcommitment, and consequent difficulties in withdrawing.

An Employee who wishes to have any involvement in a business should refer the proposition to his or her Line Executive at the earliest stage, and obtain approval in writing.

Employees with commitments entered into prior to the introduction of these guidelines should now seek the necessary approval.

(ii)   Private Interests

No Employee of the Group should assume a position, or allow a situation to arise, where there is a conflict between his or her own interests and the interests of the Group or of any customer. If this situation arises his or her Line Executive must be immediately notified of the matter. Lending or other decisions should not be taken by an Employee where there is a family relationship or connection.

(iii)   Invitations, Gifts, Payments, etc.

The receipt of invitations or the offer of any gifts, payments, services, hospitality or benefits in kind on a scale which could affect, or could be considered to affect, the ability to exercise independent judgement, should be notified, in all cases, to the Employee's Manager or Line Executive, as appropriate, and approval obtained, before any such are accepted. As it is not practical to place a Groupwide monetary value on what is acceptable, local Executive Management will, from time to time, advise Employees in their area of responsibility of invitations, gifts, etc., which may not be accepted without prior approval. Where an Employee is in any doubt as to the propriety of accepting an invitation or offer he or she should refer the matter to his or her Manager or Line Executive.

No sponsorship or gifts should be solicited or accepted for the Group, or for any event or occasion involving Group Employees, where such could be deemed to influence or compromise any business decision by the Group in relation to the sponsor or donor.

No Employee should consciously carry out any act or become involved in any situation that potentially could conflict with the principles which underlie this aspect of Group policy. However, where an Employee inadvertently finds himself or herself in any situation of difficulty under this heading, he or she is encouraged to raise the matter with his or her Manager or Head of Department, by whom the matter will be dealt with sympathetically.

4 Declaration of Secrecy

The attention of all Employees of the Group is drawn to the undertakings given by them on joining the Group. Each Employee must:

— Keep secret the affairs of the Group and its customers.

— Make known to his or her Manager, Head of Department, or Senior Line Executive, any fraud or irregularity by any Employee or customer which becomes known to him or her.

— Observe all rules and regulations of the Group.

To assist in maintaining the confidentiality of Group and customer 'market sensitive' information, Employees should only discuss such matters within the Group on a 'need-to-know' basis.

5 Employees' Financial Affairs

Employees have personal responsibility for the good order of their finances and as such are free to assume appropriate financial obligations. The spirit of these guidelines is supportive of this.

Employees' conduct of their own financial affairs should never be such as to invite comment, for instance, because of speculative transactions beyond their means or at a level which could be considered inappropriate to the position held. Employees must always be conscious of the dangers inherent in over extending themselves financially.

6 Membership of Political Parties

Personnel bulletin No. 190 dated 20th January 1987 issued to Bank Staff sets out the conditions covering membership of political parties. These are repeated here for the attention of all Group Employees.

— The Group recognises the right of an Employee to become a member of a political party subject to any such political involvement not being prejudicial to the interests of the Group.

— Any Employee who joins a political party will have a responsibility to ensure that involvement in such party is not prejudicial to the interests of the Group or creates a conflict of interests.

— It is acceptable for Employees to participate fully in political parties. This includes accepting nomination to stand in either national or local government elections. In the event of nomination and subsequent election to a national parliament, leave of absence without pay will be granted by the Group. Normally such leave of absence will be granted for up to two terms of office.

— Where canvassing arises, either on the Employee's own behalf or on behalf of other members of a political party, Employees have a special responsibility to ensure that any involvement in such canvassing is not perceived as associating the Group with any particular party. It is also important that the normal customer/Banker relationships are in no way affected, influenced or used.

8.4 ETHICAL BANKING COURSE FOR MANAGERS

It will be seen from the code of conduct that in a number of situations staff are required to refer matters to their managers. In certain cases, managers may seek advice from legal or personnel departments, but often they are expected to exercise their judgement.

The following is an example of a training course which can be adapted to suit the specific needs of any bank.

This five-day course progresses through a carefully structured sequence of steps, each of which is designed to foster the learning that will be helpful to subsequent steps. The seven main steps are:

Step 1   The forces shaping ethical banking. What this means to the role of the manager.

Step 2   Introduction to a framework or model, for thinking about causes of ethical/unethical behaviour in banking – the five canons of ethical banking.

Step 3   Exploration of the process and content of ethical decision-making, and the development of skills for thinking more adequately and effectively.

Step 4   Exploration of the origins of emotions and action planning for dealing with specific instances of one's own disruptive or self-defeating emotions.

Step 5   Exploration of some of the important influences on one's own ethical behaviour, and action planning for making any desired change in behaviour.

Step 6   Analysis of specific 'ethical problems' involving the behaviour of others in the work situation, and action planning for solving the problem.

Step 7   Analysis of own job/organisational situation and action planning for making a specific desired change.

8.4.1   Whom Does the Course Help?

The Ethical Banking Course has been designed mainly for people who have had at least two years of bank management experience. It is also appropriate for senior staff who do not manage others, but whose jobs require them to interact extensively with, and to work through, other people.

Given that a person is in one of these categories, there are several other requirements that must be met before an individual is likely to derive any benefits from the course:

(a) He should have a commitment to his continuing development and personal growth in the job he is doing.
(b) He should believe that a large part of the responsibility for learning, development and growth lies with him.
(c) He should recognise that the on-going activities of the job can provide a wealth of opportunities for learning and improving ethical decision-making and behaviour.
(d) He should recognise a need to increase his understanding of ethical banking and its implications for his future performance and growth.
(e) He should be able to identify at least one aspect of his ethical decision-making and/or behaviour which he would like to change.
(f) He should be able to identify at least one aspect of the ethical decision-making and/or behaviour of someone he works with that causes problems and which therefore he would like to change.
(g) He should be able to identify at least one aspect of his job or organisation which he would like to change in order to increase his contribution to ethical banking.

8.4.2 Why an 'Ethical Banking' Course?

A basic assumption behind the course is that a manager's capacity to improve his performance, to solve ethical problems successfully, to cope with and capitalise on change, and to learn effectively, depends on his willingness to adopt a consciously ethical approach to the way he behaves in his job. Some of the characteristics of the ethical banker's approach are:

(a) He identifies the ethical beliefs or assumptions that lie behind his choices and actions, and uses the outcomes of his choices and actions as a means of checking the validity of this ethical code.
(b) He adopts a systematic approach to ethical decision-making.
(c) If his behaviour in a particular situation has not been entirely ethical, the next time the situation occurs he behaves differently and compares the results with those previously achieved.

8.4.3 What Does a Participant Learn from the Course?

There is a strong emphasis on the course on activities in which participants generate data relevant to themselves and their job situation. They then reflect on the data to see what they can learn from it.

The responsibility for learning is therefore very much with the participants. What they learn will vary from individual to individual depending on their willingness to learn and on what is personally significant to them.

Because of this emphasis on participation it is difficult to answer the question at the head of this section in the same way as one can answer with a course more oriented to formal 'teaching'. One way of answering is to break the question into several parts:

- What is offered by the tutors to participants during this course?
  — A framework for understanding and analysing the factors which influence people's ethical behaviour.
  — Tools, techniques, activities for raising awareness of factors (such as thought processes, beliefs, values, needs) within the individual participant which influence his behaviour.
  — A theory which explains how feelings (themselves an important influence on ethical behaviour) arise and a technique for getting rid of damaging, disruptive, debilitating or self-defeating feelings.
  — Opportunities for and guidance on analysing the causes of the participants' own ethical behaviour in a defined situation, and for planning to change the behaviour in the direction of greater personal effectiveness on future occasions.
  — Opportunities for and guidance on analysing the causes of 'ethical problems', and a set of strategies which can help to resolve such problems.
  — Opportunities for planning to enhance ethical standards in the participants' zone of control and influence.

- What will participants know and what will they have done by the end of the course?
  — They will understand the five canons of ethical banking and use them to assess their behaviour and ethical decision-making.
  — They will know, and will have worked with, one framework for explaining and analysing why people behave ethically or otherwise.
  — They will know the main pitfalls to clear using effective ethical decision-making, and will have identified these in their own thought processes.
  — They will have made explicit the assumptions and beliefs they hold about some aspects of their jobs and work environment; will have reviewed where those assumptions and beliefs came

from, and will have identified those that need checking out and how they could do this.
— They will have identified the ethical values they hold on matters relevant to their work.
— They will have identified some of the important emotional needs which they have and which they attempt to satisfy at work.
— They will have identified some of the important components in the image they have of themselves.
— They will have analysed systematically the causes of a behaviour pattern of their own that they would like to change, and will have produced a plan which will help them to change it when they return to their job.
— They will have acted as 'facilitators' to their colleagues on the course in helping them to think through their ethical problems and develop plans to deal with them.

• What will participants be able to do after the course?
— They will be able to apply the five canons of ethical banking.
— They will be able to identify the likely causes of their own and others' ethical behaviour in the work situation, and to plan and take action to modify the behaviour successfully where it is appropriate to do so.
— They will be able to give more effective help to others who work for or with them to manage their feelings and ethical behaviour.

8.4.4 Course Activities

Participants spend much of the five days in activities which require individual work or working in pairs or small groups of three or four. The emphasis is on self-help, and mutual help between participants. The activities are also designed to help participants to help themselves more effectively when they return to their jobs. Formal inputs from the tutors are kept to a minimum. They are largely confined to describing the five canons of ethical banking plus models and processes which can assist participants in ethical decision-making.

Participants are encouraged to keep a personal 'learning log' through the course, in which they can reflect on, and record, learning that has been meaningful to them.

In the early steps of the course, participants use questionnaires and other analytic tools to explore a variety of aspects of themselves and their job environments which are likely to influence their feelings and ethical behaviour.

Subsequently, participants also work on specific instances of their own ethical behaviour, the ethical behaviour of others and develop action plans for appropriate change in each case.

Throughout the latter half of the course participants deal with specific instances and issues which they wish to resolve. It is important that these are issues which the individual believes are worth spending time on and can be dealt with by the participant on his return to work.

Table 8.1 gives a typical course programme.

8.5   CONTRASTING APPROACHES TO CREATING AWARENESS OF BANK CULTURE

We have seen throughout this book that ethical banking calls for commitment to a company's ethical values. This begins from the moment of joining a company or even before it, through recruitment literature.

The American giant Merrill Lynch bestrides the globe. In seeking to recruit high calibre staff it emphasises its traditional values. In a statement of its philosophy it says:

> From our earliest days, Merrill Lynch has always been run with clear ideals and high standards. We have established traditions of business behaviour which gives clients confidence and are globally consistent. Today these traditions create a sound base for all transactions.

Merrill Lynch then spells out three traditions which accord with the canons of ethical banking:

(1) The Tradition of the Customer – 'Merrill Lynch exists to respond to the needs of the customer. Institutional, corporate, government and private clients all tap different talents that the firm offers. Serving their individual and unique interests to the optimum benefit of the client is the organisation's aim.'
(2) The Tradition of Confidence – 'Finding a solution is not the same as finding the best solution. We intend every client to feel he *knows* he has received the most thorough solution and advice.'

Table 8.1   Ethical banking course for managers (sample programme)

Day 1	Introduction Forces Shaping Ethical Banking The Role of the Ethical Banker Thinking about Ethical Behaviour
Day 2	Thinking and Feelings Factors Shaping Ethical Behaviour The Canons of New Ethical Banking Canon One – Legality
Day 3	Needs and Values of Ourselves Needs and Values of Others Canon Two – Fairness The Fair Relationship (Case Studies and Role Plays) Ethical Decision-making Assessing Our Own Ethical Behaviour Changing Our Own Ethical Bahaviour
Day 4	Canon Three – Social Legitimacy The Socially Legitimate Relationship (Case Studies and Role Plays) Assessing the Ethical Behaviour of Others Influencing the Ethical Behaviour of Others Canon Four – Justification The Justifiable Relationship (Case Studies and Role Plays)
Day 5	Canon Five – Confidentiality The Confidential Relationship (Case Studies and Role Plays) Action Planning

Note: Each day can be run on a workshop basis over a period.

(3) The Tradition of Trust – 'Our commitment to the highest ethical standards remains absolute, with the future in view.'

William A. Schreyer, Chairman and Chief Executive Officer of Merrill Lynch, summarises the philosophy thus: 'A clear vision. A sound strategy. An unwavering commitment to our traditional values. These form the foundation upon which our organisation is built.' New recruits to Merrill Lynch are therefore made aware from the outset of the guiding principles which are expected to determine their ethical behaviour.

In contrast, British financial institutions are more reticent in articulating their value system. To take but two examples of highly respected companies, let us consider Lazard Brothers and Kleinwort Benson.

Lazard Brothers, whose roots go back to 1848, states that its philosophy is:

> not necessarily to be the biggest, but to be the best in the fields in which we specialised . . . We are small, successful and highly profitable . . . We are distinguished by a unique investment style pioneered by us in the USA and UK which we call 'Value'. Primarily, our aim is to invest in inexpensive shares in financially productive companies.

Lazard Brothers recruits a handful of graduates each year. The initial training consists of a tour of the bank lasting nine months. During this period graduates undertake external courses to help them in a banking career, e.g. courses in law, economics, accountancy general banking and how the City works. After that, graduates are placed in whatever area of the bank seems most suitable from their and the bank's point of view.

At no stage in its recruitment literature does Lazards mention ethical standards. This, of course, does not mean there is a lack of ethical behaviour; on the contrary, Lazard Brothers is a highly regarded company throughout the financial world. Rather it reflects the view of its American counterpart, Lazard Freres of New York Felix Rohatyn, a senior partner of that company, has said: 'I no more believe that ethics can be taught past the age of 10 than I believe in the teaching of so-called creative writing. If business students haven't been taught ethics by their families or their clergymen, a few ethics classes during business school won't make up for that neglect.'

Mr Rohatyn is entitled to his view, but as we have seen in Chapter 3, it is unlikely that children can make ethical decisions when faced with ambiguous situations. A nanny may have inculcated sound values in a child who becomes a merchant banker, but it is doubtful if she will have fully equipped him to resolve ethical dilemmas which can occur in the financial world of the 1990s.

Unlike Lazards, which is a traditional merchant bank, unchanged by the Big Bang of 1986, Kleinwort Benson is a financial group which

now embraces a wide range of activities. It recruits around twenty
graduates a year. Their training begins with a three-month programme which is tailored to 'help you meet our professional standards and succeed in the competitive business environment in which
we operate'.

The programme's objectives are to provide recruits with:

(a) A broad understanding of the structure of the City and global
    financial markets, and within that framework the role of the
    Kleinwort Benson Group.
(b) Familiarisation with the objectives, products/services and activi-
    ties of the major operating divisions.
(c) Basic financial knowledge and skills.
(d) Personal business skills.

The programme consists of a series of closely interrelated formal
classroom sessions, presentations and department visits:

— Orientation (e.g. introduction to core business activities).
— Financial knowledge and skills.
— Personal business skills.
— Visits to principal operating areas.

Although training is claimed to be a continuous process at Kleinwort
Benson, the period of formal acculturation is short. This is in common with most Western banks. By contrast, the world's largest
financial organisation, a Japanese megagiant, provides a model for
creating a deep awareness of and commitment to its culture. This
could well be adapted by those Western banks which are committed
to ethical banking.

8.6 A JAPANESE MODEL – NOMURA SECURITIES

Japanese banks adopt a long-term approach to staff training. As in
other industries, lifetime employment is the norm (as it has been until
recently in British banks). Training is perceived as an important
investment which is essential for company growth. It begins at the
company training centre which is usually residential. The recruits
share a group experience of initiation into the 'culture' of the bank
before receiving 'financial' training.

Nomura recruits around 500 new employees per year. They are sent to training centres where they share rooms, meals and, being Japan, communal baths. Bonding is encouraged together with a shared awareness of company values and ethical behaviour. Group discussions and private meetings with tutors often last well into the night.

Training in Japanese banks has a dual objective:

(1) To acquire a basic knowledge of the business.
(2) To get to know the company, its values, structure and resources.

At Nomura, in addition to basic ethical behaviour which will distinguish the individual as a 'Nomura man', each trainee must learn to master his role within the organisation.

In common with Western banks, use is made of case studies and role plays to assist the learning process. The major difference in approach comes after the formal training when individuals are assigned to their first jobs. Each is taken under the guardianship of his *senpai*, a guardian angel who acts as a benevolent mentor to the new recruit. He teaches the younger man not only the nitty gritty of his job but also reinforces adherence to the company's value system.

If the newcomer is in a sales role his *senpai* takes him on his first round of visits to clients. During his first year, the new recruit continues training, receiving visits from members of the education and training department. This not only enables the company to assess the progress of the individual, it also provides an alternative channel for the individual to voice any concerns. Training continues for a total of three years, although formal sessions will be restricted to a month or so. Nomura provides further structured training for those who have been with the company for seven years, then ten years.

One of the major differences between Nomura and its Western counterparts is that the Japanese company trains its high calibre staff to be generalists rather than specialists.

The main lessons to be learned from the Nomura approach are:

(a) Company values and ethical standards should be dealt with from the outset of training, not as an afterthought.
(b) New recruits should have close contact with a mature member of staff who can provide a model of ethical behaviour.
(c) During the training period there should be easy access to the personnel/training function which enables the trainee to voice concerns or raise issues of ethical behaviour in a non-threatening environment.

In these three respects, Japan shows the way in which to develop the new ethical banker.

8.7 TECHNIQUES FOR DEVELOPING ETHICAL AWARENESS

Codes of conduct, management training, and induction into company culture all have a role in developing ethical awareness. Other approaches which are proving useful are:

(a) Establishing end-point ethics;
(b) Agreeing standards of justice;
(c) Contrasting philosophies;
(d) Self-audits.

(a) Establishing end-point ethics is based on the work of Professor Pastin in *The Hard Problems of Management* (1988). He suggests that when faced with an ethical dilemma you should:

(1) List the different individuals or groups that your decision affects.
(2) Determine how the different choices you might make will affect them.
(3) Ask them what they think of the alternatives.
(4) Assign priorities to the parties based on both how hard they will be hit and whatever duty you owe each, whether as customers, shareholders, employees or merely fellow human beings.

Armed with this reasonably complete understanding of how each option will work, you can then decide among them. This approach can be tested privately (without the consultative phase) in considering many of the ethical dilemmas posed in this book.

(b) Standards of justice are benchmarks against which you can compare your alternative choices. For example:

— Act so as to maximise the benefit to the least advantaged in society, or at least to do them no harm.
— Act so that other people's ability to lead their lives as they wish is enhanced not limited.

(c) Contrasting philosophies create an awareness of ethical options based on a wider range of philosophies than would normally be

brought into play. This is a sophisticated technique well suited to graduates.

For example, you can consider alternative codes of conduct based on each of the following:

— Behaviourism which decrees that behaviour rather than the mind is all that can be really known about human nature and thus human conduct can only be judged in terms of what people do.
— Existentialism which claims that each of us has complete free will but no given essence; thus we have to defend ourselves by our choices in a world without ultimate moral values.
— Instrumentalism which states that the value of ideas lie in their practical success regardless of their correctness.
— Pragmatism which espouses a practical approach to personal dealings, rejecting historical or ideological factors.
— Relativism which looks on truth as not being an absolute, but varying from one person to another, from culture to culture and from age to age.
— Utilitarianism which defines the greatest good as that which produces most happiness for the greatest number of people.

By considering the consequences of these different approaches it becomes apparent that ethical banking is the result of several streams of philosophy, not just one.

(d) Self-audit: In the end ethical banking depends on individual behaviour. It is therefore useful if from time to time people are encouraged to stop and think about their actions. This is not to advocate private, or even public, confession, but simply a personal appraisal on the basis of each of the five canons. Examples of such questions are:

(1) Is what I am doing legal?
(2) Am I up to date with the relevant legislation?
(3) Is what I am doing fair to the other party?
(4) Is what I am doing likely to harm innocent people?
(5) Can I justify what I am doing?
(6) Am I in any way breaching a confidence?

There should not be a standard set of questions which may run the danger of being ignored over time. It is better to suggest different sets of questions which people may wish to use from time to time.

Discussion groups can be used to discuss Agree/Disagree exercises of the type shown in Part II. Case studies of ethical problems also provide a useful exercise for discussion groups.

8.8 CONCLUSION

Developing ethical bankers is no overnight job. It begins at the recruitment phase and continues throughout their careers. Banks need to define and implant their ethical policies and practices in much the same way as they deal with other important issues.

All aspects of ethical decision-making and behaviour cannot be codified. Management discretion and individual judgement need to be brought into play frequently. Management and staff training has a role to play here, not in 'teaching' ethics but in heightening awareness of the ethical aspects of day-to-day banking activities.

Learning to ride requires the acquisition of knowledge and skills but proficiency in riding depends not only on the rider but on the horse and their joint reaction to a situation. Similarly, in ethics there can be no examinations to be passed which will guarantee individual probity; the testing never ends. But just as it is foolhardy to put someone on a horse for the first time and expect him or her to ride proficiently, so too is it dangerous to give completely free rein to an individual to exercise judgement without having previous guidance on ethics.

9 Essential Competences for the Ethical Banker

9.1 INTRODUCTION

Ethical banking is an outcome of the many changes affecting the banking and financial services industry. The role of the banker is being reshaped as a result. A raft of new competences has to be acquired and blended with the more traditional ones of the lender.

The need for reinforcing ethical decision-making and behaviour has to be seen in terms of a kaleidoscope of changing values which Guy Dauncey, in his book *After the Crash* (1988), has classified as:

- Spiritual values
- Planetary values
- Economic values
- Ecological values
- Personal creativity values
- Local community values
- Social values

9.2 SPIRITUAL VALUES

The spiritual values are a reflection of people's growing awareness of being part of a greater whole. In ethical banking it expresses itself in terms of acknowledgement of the need for greater honesty and integrity in business. Associated with this is a shift away from blaming others for our misfortunes rather than accepting personal accountability. The deeper these values are embedded in our culture, the easier it should be for the ethical banker to be less bound by internal rules in transactions with customers. These values are closely associated with the second canon of ethical banking – fairness.

9.3 PLANETARY VALUES

The planetary values focus on Earth as a planet of interdependent parts. Investment in one part of the world which destroys livelihood in other parts is against the third canon – social legitimacy. In assessing loan applications and investment opportunities, the ethical banker needs to avoid wantonly damaging a third party. This does not mean not lending or investing, rather it asks that the banker–customer relationship, faced with issues of social legitimacy, considers alternatives and/or means of compensating those damaged by the relationship. For example, if an industrial development in area A is likely to be more profitable than in area B where the industry is currently located, some of the profits from the new enterprise in area A might be channelled to area B to enable it to develop new industries.

9.4 ECONOMIC VALUES

These represent the economic values of efficiency and profitability. While profit is essential for survival, the focus on economic values exclusively can be destructive.

Whereas the traditional canons of lending concentrate almost exclusively on the economic values of a proposal for a loan, the ethical banker applies a wider spectrum of values in considering the efficacy of a loan application.

As society acknowledges a range of values in judging ethical behaviour, the fourth canon of ethical banking – justification – comes into play. No longer can a decision to lend, invest or gather in money be considered solely in terms of economic values; the ethical banker must be prepared to reach and justify decisions against more varied criteria.

9.5 ECOLOGICAL VALUES

The past decade has witnessed an extraordinary acceleration of the importance of applying sound ecological values to all investment decisions. Pressure groups and mainstream politicians have combined to ensure that manufacturers and retailers have taken the necessary steps to reduce and, where possible, eliminate damage to the environment. This accords with the first and third canons of ethical banking.

In a sense there is a need for a new canon of lending – ecological acceptability. The ethical banker who does not take full account of the potential ecological effects of any new or recurrent request for a loan is courting economic damage for his bank. Similarly, the investment of savers' funds must also be treated with ecological sensitivity, as well as political sensitivity.

9.6 CREATIVITY AND FULFILMENT VALUES

These values provide banking with external opportunities and internal threats. People want to have more opportunities to express their creativity and to feel a sense of fulfilment in their work. This is reflected in the spread of 'freedom to manage' which is being encouraged in many banks.

The ethical banker can, through judicious lending, help customers to profit from their creativity and gain fulfilment through individual and cooperative ventures. This ability of banking to increase the stretch of human ambition so that dreams can be realised sooner is a concept which banks need to communicate more effectively. New products to finance 'craft cooperatives' and 'creative networks' will increasingly be in demand.

However, the very values which create opportunities in the marketplace will cause tension in the workplace. Bank employees will seek increasing opportunities to be creative and fulfilled. 'Empowerment' will become a growing force in the personnel armoury of banks. Empowerment without training and guidance can lead to anarchy. If managers have not acquired the necessary competences, freedom to manage becomes freedom to mismanage.

9.7 LOCAL COMMUNITY VALUES

Local/global banks will be a feature of the banking industry from now on. The growth in bank mergers and increasing international linkages is changing the geographical spread of banks. For example, people in most Yorkshire towns in the 1990s can choose to be customers of an Australian owned bank (Yorkshire) or one that is partly Hong Kong owned (Midland), as distinct from British banks.

For most customers, their primary focus is on the local rather than the global activities of their bank. There is an increasing desire by people to identify with local communities. Initiatives such as Neighbourhood Watch, Meals on Wheels, community centres and local radio stations are all reflections of this trend. The challenge for the ethical banker is to be part of the local community whilst responding to the more global demands, targets and aspirations of 'the bank'.

9.8 SOCIAL VALUES

Dominating all the other values discussed so far are social values. These reflect concern for justice, compassion, equality of treatment and opportunity. The elimination of racial, sexual and religious prejudice is an uphill task in which the ethical banker has an important role to play. By their nature, banks tend to be conservative since they have legal and moral obligations to safeguard the monies of others. However, as we saw in Chapter 2, the new social values are bringing into the forefront new types of banking. Established banks can either adapt to the changes in social values and survive and prosper or they can resist the waves of change, Canute-like, and face the consequences.

9.9 NEW CHALLENGES

The changing value systems will provide the ethical framework within which the ethical banker needs to cope with the new challenges facing every bank in the 1990s:

- Cost containment/reduction;
- Realigning markets;
- Enhancing service quality;
- Managing technology;
- Exploring new business alliances;
- Stimulating innovation;
- Encouraging greater ethical awareness.

All these call for proficiency in a range of competences. Traditional competences will continue to play a critical role in the effectiveness of bank managers, regardless of their role, and will include:

— Leadership
— Team building
— Communications

— Interviewing
— Communication skills
— Computer literacy
— Marketing skills
— Negotiating skills
— Financial analysis

In addition to these traditional skills there are emerging new competences which arise from:

(a) Ethical awareness;
(b) The need for greater strategic awareness in management thinking;
(c) A more precise definition of individual accountabilities;
(d) A more rigorous assessment of performance;
(e) Fewer and slimmer support departments;
(f) Increasing flexibility in manpower;
(g) More openness in communications.

These competences and how best to develop them are described in detail in the training grids in Tables 9.1 to 9.5. Before turning to them let us consider the new challenges.

9.10 COST CONTAINMENT/REDUCTION

The competences required for cost containment/reduction are:

— a familiarity with cost management options
    cost–benefit analysis
    cost-effectiveness
    budgeting control;
— the ability to convince subordinates of the need for belt-tightening even in times of improved profitability;
— flexibility in the allocation of resources;
— resilience in resisting pressures for overriding budgets;
— a willingness to dispose of sacred cows.

Keeping a tight rein on costs while being responsive to market opportunities is no easy task. A careful balance has to be maintained between stewardship and intransigence.

This calls for training in such subjects as:

(a) Budgeting
(b) Cost management
(c) Problem solving
(d) Communications
(e) Team-building

Decisions on cost reduction will raise ethical issues which must be tested against the canons of ethical banking and discarded if found wanting.

9.11   REALIGNING MARKETS

Realigning markets involves strategic withdrawal from the unprofit-able, counterbalanced by greater penetration into the potentially profitable. This requires a management style that is:

(1) Strategically aware – able to anticipate customer needs and expectations.
(2) Adept at empathising with both the 'discarded' and the attractive market segments.
(3) Highly visible to customers and staff.
(4) Responsive to changing demands.
(5) Proficient in risk assessment.

The critical performance factor is to balance flexibility with persist-ence; running after every new development in the market can be as dangerous as not moving at all. There is, therefore, a need for training in such subjects as:

— Market analysis;
— Presentation skills;
— Selling skills;
— Trust-building.

Once again, ethical considerations will arise, particularly in with-drawing from previous markets. The canons will provide guidance in resolving ethical dilemmas.

9.12   ENHANCING SERVICE QUALITY

Service quality is being recognised as the most sustainable competitive differentiation. While products, pricing and, to a lesser degree, premises will continue to be competitive weapons, when these are matched by rivals, customers will opt for the bank which provides them with the best service experience. The service experience has to be 'managed' at all levels, for without a deeply entrenched 'service quality culture' it is not possible to sustain a customer service differentiation.

My research into a variety of financial service institutions suggests that the raft of changes which has impacted on the industry in recent years has given rise to two conflicting cultures – a culture of resentment and a culture of achievement. Basically, the culture of resentment stems from a sense of frustration born of low self-esteem in the face of changing demands ('I didn't join the bank to be a salesman'). The culture of achievement looks on change as a motivating challenge. The characteristics are listed in Table 9.6.

Managing the shift from resentment to achievement requires a management style which is characterised by:

— the ability to stimulate enthusiasm for the stated mission;
— the ability to engender openness and to build trust;
— the motivating and coaching of skills necessary for empowering people to overcome their fear of failure and strive for optimum performance.

Such management style will not be imparted by a training course. However, training in the broader sense of self-development, coaching, assignments and secondments all have a part to play. In designing the appropriate learning experiences there will be a need to recognise the growing importance of 'lattice management' – the ability to manage upwards, sideways, and diagonally as well as downwards. Lattice management will be the key to drawing on the various specialists needed in financial services in the 1990s.

9.13   MANAGING TECHNOLOGY

A distinction has to be drawn between the specialist manager in technology and the branch/department manager who uses technology. This section is concerned with the latter.

Computer literacy and keyboard proficiency will continue to be a requirement for all managers. In addition, technology will provide the hub for enhanced effectiveness in:

(a) Cost containment/reduction;
(b) Marketing;
(c) Service quality.

A growing training need will be managing the workflow in a manner that improves productivity and quality. Specific management training needs will include:

(1) Workflow charting and analysis techniques;
(2) Project definition;
(3) Project planning and organisation;
(4) Scheduling/contingency planning.

9.14 EXPLORING NEW BUSINESS ALLIANCES

The advent of the Single European Act, the changing legislative framework in the USA, and the growth of global corporations are among the forces leading banks to seek new alliances for all or part of their operations. While the numbers of managers engaged in the exploration and negotiations will be small, the impact of any merger or other arrangement will be widespread.

This trend will call for high levels of strategic and negotiating skills for those directly involved. As far as the generality of managers is concerned, there should be built into courses:

— Awareness of global trends;
— Managing change.

For those involved in actual mergers there should be training in avoiding 'merger drift' – the tendency for energy to be dissipated before and after mergers by focusing on internal politics rather than on serving the market.

9.15 STIMULATING INNOVATION

In the increasingly competitive markets of the 1990s there will be a growing demand by customers for 'added value'. The response to these demands is likely to be threefold:

(1) improved service quality;
(2) improved products;
(3) improved delivery systems.

In each case, managers will have to exhibit and stimulate innovation. Encouraging creativity will call for many of the skills already cited. In addition, there will have to be:

(a) a higher tolerance for creative mavericks;
(b) gainsharing by the innovators;
(c) an acceptance of tolerable levels of failure;
(d) encouragement of risk taking.

History has shown that many banks have put a heavy investment into this area of training with limited benefit. This may have been due to the lack of a culture in which the training could take root; another factor could have been the nature of the training, some of which appeared gimmicky. This needs to be avoided in training plans. Management training is intended to convert rather than divert.

9.16 ENCOURAGING GREATER ETHICAL AWARENESS

Throughout this book we have dealt with this subject and identified the key competences which managers need to develop if ethical standards are to be enhanced:

- Advisory skills;
- Trust-building;
- Acceptance of criticism;
- Empowerment of staff to make ethical decisions.

Advisory skills will include:

(1) *Counselling* – a style of helping which will give the customer a

sense of personal security through sympathetic listening and empathy.

2) *Advising* – developing options and getting the customer to select the one he/she favours.

3) *Confronting* – challenging the customer to examine how the present foundation of their thinking on financial matters may be based on mistaken assumptions.

4) *Prescribing* – telling the customer what to do to rectify a situation.

The essential basis for advisory skills to work are openness and trust. There are two aspects to openness:

— a mutual sharing of data and exchange of views;
— a willing receptivity to new ideas and experiences.

When it comes to trust-building there are three prerequisites:

1) integrity in relationships;
2) credibility in performance;
3) consistency in behaviour.

Acceptance of criticism does not come easily to any of us. But ethical banking demands that criticism be encouraged, not stifled. Managers need help in handling criticism and managing any resulting disagreement constructively. This calls for mastering a process of:

a) Diagnosing the causes of the criticism;
b) Planning to remove the causes or communicate more clearly the reasons;
c) Preparing a course of remedial action;
d) Implementing the action;
e) Evaluating the results.

Empowerment of staff to take ethical decisions requires adopting the policies and practices covered in Chapter 8.

9.17   CONCLUSION

Banking is operating in a world of changing values, politics and technology. The banker in the 1990s needs to be equipped with both sound ethical values and a range of competences.

New challenges face the banking and financial services industry. To meet and conquer these challenges will call for a reappraisal of training methods with a focus on competence building.

Table 9.1 Self-management competences training grid (traditional competences)

Competency	Definition	Knowledge required	Best acquired by	Skills required	Best acquired by
Decision-making	Capacity to determine objectives, having identified alternatives to their achievement and assessed the risk relating to each alternative.	Process of decision-making (individual) Processes of decision-making (groups) Techniques of problem solving	Reading Exercises Observation Feedback	Synthesising different subjects Maze brightness Prioritising	Projects Action learning Case studies Self-development Outward bound
Problem solving	Capacity to resolve the demands of a situation which will lead to the optimum outcome.	Techniques of situation analysis Techniques of creativity	Reading Exercises Observation Feedback	Ability to précis Statistical analysis Prioritising	Projects Action learning Case studies Self-development Outward bound
Time management	Capacity to allocate the requisite time to accomplishing diverse tasks and consistently to meet deadlines.	Awareness of own capacities Deadlines	Self-analysis Feedback Interviewing	Diarising Prioritising Planning	Projects Self-development Exercises

(continued on page 160)

Table 9.1 *continued* (New competences)

Competency	Definition	Knowledge required	Best acquired by	Skills required	Best acquired by
Assertiveness	Capacity to stand up for one's own rights without violating the rights of others.	Procedures for decision-making Logical thinking Techniques of persuasiveness	Self-analysis Tests Feedback Reading	Debating Persuading Empathising	Role plays Projects Action learning Self-development
Personal effectiveness	Capacity to blend one's strengths in an optimum manner which will achieve a sought objective.	Self-awareness of strengths and weaknesses	Self-analysis Tests Feedback	Self-presentation Empathising Goal setting Persuading	Exercises Role plays Feedback
Stress management	Capacity to absorb pressure, to exert tolerable pressure on others, to identify signs of strain in self and others.	Basic psychology Strengths and weaknesses of self and others Situation analysis	Self-analysis Reading Tests Discussion	Communication Persuading Empathising Interviewing	Projects Self-development Simulations Role plays

Table 9.2 People management competences training grid (traditional competences)

Competency	Definition	Knowledge required	Best acquired by	Skills required	Best acquired by
Appraising	Capacity to apply the appraisal system in a manner which will bring about the desired change in the performance of appraisees.	Appraisal objectives and process Performance standards and measures Data on appraisees	Workshop on appraisal system On-job performance analysis Review of personal file and performance results	Interviewing Listening Checking understanding Persuading Objective-setting	Workshop on appraisal system Regular contact with appraisees
Communicating	Capacity to transmit views, instructions, and ideas in a manner which is understood and acted on correctly by those concerned.	Vocabulary Verbal and non-verbal means of communicating	Reading Courses	Writing Speaking Verbal and non-verbal presentation	Courses Projects Action learning

(continued on page 162)

Table 9.2 continued

Competency	Definition	Knowledge required	Best acquired by	Skills required	Best acquired by
Counselling	Capacity to help others talk about, explore and understand their problems and to decide on their own solutions.	Basic psychology	Reading	Questioning Reflecting back views Listening	Practising interviewing Role-playing
Delegating	Capacity to assign authority to others to achieve objectives, whilst retaining accountability for results.	Results to be achieved Capabilities of delegatees	Self-development Projects	Target-setting Communicating Performance monitoring Trust-building	Self-development Case studies Role-playing Action learning
Interviewing	Capacity to question individuals in a manner which elicits responses on which decisions on subsequent action can be made.	Personal and situational factors relevant to interview	Self-development Reading Observation	Questioning Listening	Practice Role plays

Leadership*	Capacity to select the appropriate type of authority, motivation and communications to blend the needs of individuals, the group and the tasks involved in achieving objectives.	Alternative leadership styles, Methods of motivation	Lectures, Reading, Action learning	Identifying the main factors in a situation, Communicating objectives, Follow through	Case studies, Role plays, Projects
Motivating	Capacity to engender in others a willingness to act in a way which will achieve prescribed objectives.	Basic psychology, Theories of motivation	Reading, Discussion	Identification of motivators, Selection of appropriate motivator, Communication of requirements, Feedback	Role-playing, Simulations, Case studies, Self-development, Projects

* Is essentially an amalgam of competencies; but some argue that it is a distinctive competency, hence its inclusion.

(continued on page 164)

Table 9.2 continued

Competency	Definition	Knowledge required	Best acquired by	Skills required	Best acquired by
Negotiating	Capacity to reach agreement which is mutually beneficial despite the existence of conflicting factors.	Negotiating styles Self-awareness Relevant data on opponent	Reading Discussion Self-development	Objective-setting Selection of appropriate negotiating style Timing	Projects Action learning Simulations e.g. team role plays
Running meetings	Capacity to conduct meetings in a manner which will enable participants to contribute fully to achieving the objective for which the meeting has been convened.	Agenda setting Group dynamics Data on participants Methods of persuasion	Reading Simulations Lectures	Discussion leading Chairmanship Summarising Listening	Simulations Role plays Action learning

Team-building	Capacity to draw out the appropriate competences of individuals, combining them in a synergistic manner which will achieve the shared objective.	Group dynamics Team roles	Reading Lectures	Discussion leading Synergising Delegating	Simulations Role-playing Action learning
Training/ coaching	Capacity to enhance the learning capability and performance of individuals through guidance and instruction.	Principles of learning Training methods Principles of counselling	Reading Lectures	Giving instructions Empathising Listening Motivating	Role-playing Simulations Distance learning

(continued on page 166)

Table 9.2   continued   (New competences)

Competency	Definition	Knowledge required	Best acquired by	Skills required	Best acquired by
Consensus-building	Capacity to gain commitment of diverse interests to an agreed course of action.	Personality types Techniques of persuasion Data on participants	Reading Lectures Videos	Persuasiveness Behaviour analysis Listening	Self-development Simulations Role plays
Human resourcing	Capacity to identify human resource implications of business plans and deploy people accordingly.	Business planning Manpower forecasting techniques Specific plans	Lectures Simulations Reading	Statistical analysis Presentation of data	Simulations Projects

Human risk-taking	Capacity to support unconventional approaches to achieving goals.	Techniques of creativity Individual assessment Man/job matching	Reading Simulations	Personnel selection Communicating ideas Delegating Empowering	Reading Simulations Role plays Projects Self-development
Matrix management	Capacity to exercise power and influence vertically, horizontally, and diagonally.	Principles of organisation Structure of the bank Techniques of persuasion	Reading Lectures Experience	Persuasive skills Ability to synthesise diverse activities	Role plays Projects Action learning Self-development
Trust/building	Capacity to foster trust in all relationships and to encourage openness.	Business psychology Trust reinforcers Barriers to trust	Reading Self-development Discussion	Listening Empathising Influencing	Case studies Simulations Role plays Projects Action learning

Table 9.3 Systems management competences training grid (traditional competences)

Competency	Definition	Knowledge required	Best acquired by	Skills required	Best acquired by
Computer literacy	Capacity to understand and explain the basic functions of a computer.	Basic components of a computer Basic computer language Fundamentals of programming Relevance of the computer to the role	Reading Distance learning Lectures	Use of keyboard Writing a simple programme	Demonstration Practice Feedback
Information skills	Capacity to: Identify the interdependence of data and information flows. Devise surveys and other devices for gathering relevant data. Transform 'chunks' of raw data into relevant information for decision-taking.	Information systems within the bank Interpretation, analysis and classification of data	Reading Projects	Establishing a data bank Skimming of data Translation of raw data into information which can be acted on	Demonstration Projects Tests
Work-flow management	Capacity to chart, analyse and schedule optimum work loads which are interdependent.	Work-flow analysis Basics of organisation and methods Basics of operational research CWIP (clerical work improvement programme)	Reading Projects Demonstration	Charting work-flow Timing Application of CWIP	Lectures Demonstrations Distance learning Tests

Table 9.4 Business management competences training grid (traditional competences)

Competency	Definition	Knowledge required	Best acquired by	Skills required	Best acquired by
Budgeting	Capacity to estimate future pattern of income and/or expenditure accurately.	Principles of financial forecasting Principles of costing	Reading Distance learning	Estimating flows of income/ expenditure Assessing time spans for achieving objectives Presentation of financial data	Demonstration Testing Self-development Projects Distance learning
Controlling	Capacity to identify critical signals governing operation of business systems and processes.	Principles of financial control Indicators of business success/ problems	Reading Distance learning Case studies	Establishing standards and measures of performance Interpreting signals of change Exercising balanced controls	Lectures Case studies Projects Distance learning
Evaluating	Capacity to judge the pros and cons of business options and to measure outcomes of the chosen option.	Techniques of business evaluation Decision-taking by individuals and groups	Case studies Reading Distance learning	Judgement Decision-making Objective setting	Case studies Projects Self-development Distance learning

(continued on page 170)

170

Table 9.4 continued

Competency	Definition	Knowledge required	Best acquired by	Skills required	Best acquired by
Planning	Capacity to establish a hierarchy of objectives and to determine the sequencing of events and allocation of resources necessary for their achievement.	Forecasting of trends Principles of objective setting Determining options Principles of estimating	Reading Lectures Case studies Testing	Use of forecasting techniques Estimating Interpretation of trends Presentation of proposals	Demonstration Projects Action learning Distance learning Self-development
		(New competences)			
Business case-making	Capacity to make a case in business terms for embarking on a particular course of action.	Principles of business analysis Critical factors in specific businesses	Reading Case studies Distance learning	Presentation skills Communicating Empathising Simplifying complex concepts	Courses Projects Case studies Self-development
Change management	Capacity to map out a change programme; identify sources of resistance; gain the commitment of those involved in overcoming the resistances and implementing the desired cha...	Environmental trends Characteristics of organisational change Techniques of persuasion	Reading Action learning Projects Self-development	Objective setting Communicating Team-building Persuading Flexibility	Projects Self-development Action learning

Cost management	Capacity to manage costs in a flexible manner, optimising cost effectiveness within budgetary limits.	Budgets Sources of cost Cost–benefit analysis Principles of cost effectiveness	Lectures Reading Distance learning	Communicating Analysis of cost structures Anticipation of cost trends	Lectures Projects Distance learning Case studies
Ethical judgement	Capacity to ensure that all transactions are conducted within the appropriate laws and in accordance with the moral standards of the bank.	Financial laws and regulations Ethical standards of the bank	Lectures Reading Distance learning	Risk assessment Character judgement Moral judgement	Case studies Role plays Action learning
Profit management	Capacity to identify the profit potential of an activity and to realise that potential.	Profit margins and contributions of all relevant products and services Principles of financial control	Reading Case studies	Objective setting Monitoring performance Cross-selling Packaging a product/service	Distance learning Projects Action learning Courses Simulations
Project management	Capacity to coordinate diverse resources in developing and implementing an action programme.	Principles of project planning Group dynamics	Lectures Case studies Distance learning	Objective setting Coordinating Communicating Motivating	Projects Self-development Case studies Simulations

(continued on page 172)

Table 9.4 continued

Competency	Definition	Knowledge required	Best acquired by	Skills required	Best acquired by
Quality management	Capacity to ensure that the performance standards are met for the delivery of services; to set and adhere to new standards as necessary.	Principles of quality assurance Standard setting Measures of quality	Reading Lectures Distance learning	Controlling quality Setting standards and measures Motivating	Projects Self-development Action learning Distance learning
Service management	Capacity to manage the service experience of customers in a manner which meets their needs and exceeds their expectations.	Concepts of service design and delivery	Lectures Reading Case studies	Anticipating customer needs and expectations Motivating Communicating	Case studies Simulations Projects Self-development

173

Table 9.5 Strategic management competences training grid (new competences)*

Competency	Definition	Knowledge required	Best acquired by	Skills required	Best Acquired by
Environmental scanning	Capacity to monitor external trends, identify and interpret 'signals' of change.	Current trends affecting financial services. Techniques of forecasting	Reading Lectures	Interpretation of trends. Determination of impact of trends	Lectures Case studies Projects Self-development
Global perception	Capacity to see the 'whole picture' in a given situation.	Interaction of internal and external changes. Situation analysis	Reading Lectures Distance learning	Integration of diverse factors to create a whole. Holistic thinking	Case studies Projects
Vision sharing	Capacity to articulate the 'vision' of the bank, where unit fits in, and to gain commitment to the vision.	Bank strategies	Reading	Communicating Motivating Listening	Workshops Action learning

Note:
* These are a breakdown of the traditional competency, 'Strategic thinking'.

Table 9.6   Characteristics of the culture of resentment and the culture of achievement

Resentment	Achievement
Backward looking	Forward looking
Retains negative feelings	Shares success
Low self-esteem	High self-esteem
Frustration	Openness
Takes satisfaction from the	Trust
failure of others	Cooperative competition
Grapevine focuses on bad news	Pride in contribution
Combative competition	Proactive
Grudging contribution	

10 Surviving in an Age of Default

10.1 INTRODUCTION

The concept of 'reciprocal obligation' lies at the heart of ethical banking. When a bank fails to abide by this concept it moves into the murky world of usury. When a customer fails to respect the concept, the bank is drawn into the swamps of liquidation and bankruptcy. The very word 'bankruptcy' is redolent of an undesirable state of affairs, a lack of some desirable quality.

The S & L fiasco in the United States in the 1980s and the failure of secondary banking in London in the 1970s show that 'banks' can themselves become bankrupt. Financial bankruptcy is easily identifiable; there are well-established accounting and legal procedures for dealing with its consequences. Ethical bankruptcy is more difficult to deal with. It creeps up insidiously on individuals and companies. Pressure to 'mind one's own business' leads to blinkered vision, the turning of the head when misdemeanours occur.

Misdemeanours not dealt with lead to mishaps, fraud, theft and corruption. Be it a state, a corporation or a bank branch, tolerance for unethical behaviour leads to more unethical behaviour. History shows that where a society tolerates defaulting on taxes, the law abiding taxpayer eventually joins the ranks of the defaulting taxpayers; so it is with banks and their customers. Stemming the tide of default and eventually turning it away has to be done by banks themselves, otherwise the contagion will spread.

10.2 COPING WITH DEFAULT

The basis of the canons of ethical banking is to educate the customer so that he or she can work with the bank manager on the principle of reciprocal obligation. This means that bankers and their staff need to be knowledgeable not only about products and procedures, but also the psychic aspect of customer needs and expectations. Customer care has to become not simply an aid to marketing, but a day-to-day reality.

CARE can be spelt out in various ways. There are three dimensions of customer care which can be brought into play in coping with default. First there is the 'People' dimension:

- *C*apture hearts and minds.
- *A*dd value to every customer experience.
- *R*each out to help.
- *E*mpower people to show that the company cares.

By itself the people dimension will not reinforce ethical banking. There are also the 'product' and procedural aspects. CARE in terms of 'product' design and development means:

- *C*onstantly search out customer needs and expectations.
- *A*dd value greater than the competition.
- *R*enew product through innovation.
- *E*nsure value for money.

CARE in relation to 'procedures' needs to be spelt out differently:

- *C*heck that the right things are being done in the right way.
- *A*djust swiftly to changing circumstances.
- *R*eview progress against goals.
- *E*xplore new ways of enhancing customer care.

Bank managers' predilection for golf should help them to think of themselves as 'inverse golfballs': flexible on the outside, but firm within. Perhaps the most necessary characteristic of bankers in the caring 1990s will be 'tough care'; the ability to show care and concern in a realistic manner. The development and training of bank managers as described in Chapters 8 and 9 will help to develop and sustain 'tough care'.

10.3 MASTERING DEFAULT

Customers default on their obligations to lenders for one or more of the following reasons, each of which has to be dealt with:

- *Fraud* – this is a criminal matter for prosecution by the police.
- *Incompetence* – this is a fault in risk assessment on the part of the

lender; it can be cured by effective training.
- *Ignorance or misunderstanding of financial processes and obliga-tions* – this is a fault in educating the customer and/or monitoring progress. Each business has a different operating/profit cycle, yet each customer is subject to a cycle of review designed for the convenience of bank reporting rather than the characteristic of the business concerned.
- *Change in the business climate* – this means that despite their best efforts, companies may not be able to adjust to changing markets and economic upheavals.
- *Changes in personal circumstances* – sickness, death of a key partner, growing old, are all circumstances which can adversely affect the capacity of a company to survive.

Added to this traditional list is *social tolerance of default*.

In Britain the 1990s began with protests and riots against the newly introduced Community Charge or Poll Tax. Failure to pay the Charge became a matter of social pride. The flames of tax default were fanned by political firebrands. But these flames were not quenched because many people of all political persuasions felt the tax to be iniquitous. The forces of law are unable to master default in Scotland, England and Wales. In Northern Ireland, a history of default – 'Can't pay; won't pay' – dissuaded the Government from even introducing the Community Charge into that part of the United Kingdom.

More sinister for banks and building societies than defaulting Community Charge payers are defaulting mortgage borrowers. Arrears in paying mortgage instalments is at an unprecedented rate. An analysis of the reasons for this type of default gives clues as to how to master this type of unethical behaviour.

A major cause of the arrears phenomenon is economic. Sustained high interest rates led borrowers to prop up their financial needs with further borrowing against the value of their property. Building societies eager to use their new lending powers were all too willing to lend on the basis of property without taking the canons of lending fully into their risk assessment.

Borrowings against property grew at the very time when property values were declining. Mortgagors have discovered increasingly that the value of their property is less than the loan outstanding. Home ownership, the road to riches through capital appreciation, has become the road to ruin.

Mortgage lenders have no desire to repossess property which is declining in value, hence the growth of debt counselling – often a case of too little, too late. Customer education should come before debt is incurred, not at the end of the road.

A second factor influencing the arrears situation was the fact that, over the last twenty-five years in Britain, houses have been bought as places to sell for tax-free gain rather than as places to live. Associated with this have been borrowings to finance such embellishments as swimming pools, conservatories, flood lighting, not to make the house more of a home but more of a selling proposition. Suddenly the 'extras' are only extra financial burdens. People feel cheated, misled, let down – the Government may be blamed but it cannot be removed, so the finger of fault is directed at the lender.

Matters are made worse as customers read of banks writing off many millions in loans to major companies, rescuing multimillion-aires, spending lavishly on new offices, staff uniforms, refurbished premises. And so a new species of borrower has come into being. The ranks of the 'Can't pay; won't pay' social and political malcontents have been joined by the 'Can pay; but why pay?' respectable middle classes.

What is to be done?

As discussed earlier in the book, banks, and all other financial institutions, need to:

- Anticipate trends likely to affect them (Chapter 2).
- Articulate and inculcate a commitment to ethical banking practices at all levels (Chapter 3).
- Involve customers more positively in the delivery process (Chapter 4).
- Add value to every customer experience (Chapters 5, 6 and 7).
- Develop the competences of bankers to enable them not simply to be providers of finance and financial advice, but to be trusted counsellors, even if it is spelt coun-*sellers* (Chapters 8 and 9).

10.4 ADDING VALUE THROUGH ETHICAL BANKING

The most important weapon in the hands of ethical bankers in an age of default is creating added-value. By this means they will gain the support of decent customers, avoid the interference of politicians and satisfy the regulators. Ways of adding value will include:

- Passing on to customers the benefits of economies of scale and automation. This means conveying to customers that mergers, reorganisation and innovation are in *their* interest as well as in the interest of the bank.
- Putting right a wrong swiftly and in a spirit of good will, rather than conveying a sense of reluctant conformance.
- Conveying a feeling that the customer being dealt with is the 'only customer' at that point in time.
- Making regular, conforming customers feel that it is worthwhile being regular and conforming to the principle of reciprocal obligation.
- Recognising a customer's good idea and rewarding it.

10.5 FIVE SIGNPOSTS TO THE FUTURE

There are five signposts on the road to ethical banking. Each will present new challenges and provide the means of conquering default.

The first is to educate customers so that they will be aware of what financial services can do and can't do. While employee education will remain important, customer education will become vital in three areas:

- Creating a positive understanding of the role which banking and financial services make to social well-being.
- Heightening awareness of the nature of data which is required from customers to enable banks to respond to their needs and expectations.
- Guiding customers on how to make the best use of bank technology in order to meet their costs effectively.

The customer has to be brought into the service delivery process, not simply when using an ATM but at all points of delivery. This leads on to the second signpost – reaching out to the customer.

In the 1990s, technology will play an increasing role in banking; unless well managed, this can lead to technology alienation. To offset this, bank managers and staff will have to be more willing to visit customers. Since there is a limit to the mobility of branch managers a new model of customer care will emerge based on the medical profession:

- Branch managers will become more like general practitioners, with a morning 'surgery' followed by a schedule of visits to customers and potential customers.
- 'Specialists' will be available to assist the branch manager in 'counselling'.
- Branch staff will act as 'para-medics', showing care for all and 'tough care' for those who are in danger of defaulting.

Eventually, in a world of advanced telecommunications, a bank can meet the needs of the customer without having a branch network. The few remaining branches might become 'commitment centres' where staff and management will meet from time to time for renewal and training in ethical banking.

The third signpost is the need to manage technology lapses. The unfulfilled technology promises of the 1980s will become the reality of the 1990s. The driving force will be ecology as much as technology. Paper will become increasingly expensive; its waste through mistakes and advertising gimmicks will no longer be tolerated. However, total dependency on VDUs will call for changes in the behaviour of both bankers and customers:

- Speed of communication by electronic mail will increase expectations of speed of response.
- 'Virus' attacks on computers will pose constant threats to the accuracy of data.
- 'Hackers' will provide a pathway to fraud.
- Customers will be segmented in terms of computer literacy or illiteracy, with the latter paying higher charges.

The main challenge to ethical banking presented by this signpost will be the occurrence of lapses and catastrophe. No technology system can be guaranteed to provide perpetual and total reliability. Systems will fail, phantom withdrawals from ATMs will occur. Where a lapse occurs its consequences should be anticipated and practices established to manage the situation in a manner which will be perceived as ethical. Too often when a system fails, the innocent victims are both the bank and its customer; however, it is the customer who appears to be victimised. This can lead to a tolerance for default in customers supporting their fellow victims.

The fourth signpost is: conveying the personal touch. The desire for personalised service will grow apace in the 1990s. Andy Warhol's prediction of '10 minutes' celebrity for everyone' may not become a literal reality, but it highlights the desire of people to feel they are receiving 'something special' which makes them believe that they are 'someone special'. The bank which makes its customers feel good about themselves will also make them feel good about the bank. This, in turn, will reinforce their commitment to the principle of reciprocal obligation.

The challenge is to transform customers into 'advocates' – espousing the merits of dealing with 'their' bank. Ways in which this can be done might include:

- Offering 'free extras' which cost little but make a big psychic impact.
- Providing 'lifestyle financial packages' which convey a sense of 'just for you'.
- Helping potential defaulters to deal with the situation before it is too late.

The final signpost – mutual trust – is what this book has been about. The entreaty 'Trust me' has been the sobriquet of the charlatan through the ages. Ethical banking provides a more solid foundation than a form of words. It is a way of living, not a way of talking. The various exercises and the moral dilemmas in Part II have been designed to help in this process of self-awareness and renewal. The situations described may appear mundane, not intellectually challenging, focusing too much on dealing with 'small fry'. However, when it comes to matters of ethics we are normally trying to cope with day-to-day matters, intelligence is no substitute for moral fibre; dealing effectively with 'small fry' will help to avoid being burnt by 'big fry'.

So, as you ponder on the dilemmas and exercises, bear in mind one thought: ethical banking without profit is philanthropy; profit without ethical banking is theft.

Part II

Discussion Exercises and Problems

The following exercises and problems are designed to stimulate ethical awareness and improve ethical decision-making. They can be used on an individual or team basis on training courses or group discussions. The problems can be adapted as role plays as well as being used as case studies.

11 Discussion Exercises

11.1 GENERAL ETHICAL ISSUES

First, on your own, read the following statements and mark whether you agree or disagree. Then go through the statements again with your colleagues and discuss where your views differ. In each case where you differ, draw up criteria which would be acceptable to all the group as a basis for ethical behaviour.

Agree | **Disagree**

1. It is always wrong to break the law.

2. It is always wrong to tell a lie.

3. It is always wrong to take any advantage of another's ignorance.

4. It is always wrong to discriminate in your treatment of people on the basis of their sex, race, colour, creed.

5. It is always wrong to withhold information which others have the right to know.

6. It is always wrong to accept praise which is equally deserved by others of whom the praiser is unaware.

7. It is always right to inform the appropriate authorities of the malpractices of others regardless of the consequences.

8. It is always right to come to the defence of someone whom you believe is being unjustly treated regardless of the consequences.

9. It is always right to resign on a matter of principle.

10. It is always wrong to betray a confidence.

11.2   BUSINESS PRACTICES – ETHICAL OR UNETHICAL?

First on your own, read the following statements and mark whether you agree or disagree. Then go through the statements again with your colleagues and discuss those where your views differ. In each case where you differ, draw up criteria which would be acceptable to all the group as a basis for ethical behaviour.

Agree | Disagree

1. It is unethical to withhold relevant information from a colleague to help you win a case.

2. It is unethical to withhold relevant information from a customer to help you make a sale.

3. It is unethical purposely to spring a proposed unpopular course of action 'at the last minute' to reduce the risks of opposition.

4. It is unethical to use the technique, 'If I do not hear from you by such a date I will assume you agree', if you know it will be difficult for the other party to meet your deadline.

5. It is unethical to leave an important piece of information on the desk of a colleague in the hope it will not be seen by him/her before you act upon it.

6. It is unethical to circumvent an agreement to give 48 hours notice of a proposed change by issuing such a notice on a Friday and implementing the change on Monday.

7. It is unethical to use ambiguous statements in advertising a product or service. For example, '24 hour service' is interpreted by the company as, 'Service will be provided within 24 hours of requests received during normal opening hours.'

8. It is unethical to use specialist jargon to conform to legal obligations to keep customers informed of their rights.

Agree | Disagree

9. It is unethical to post at the cheapest rates information which customers urgently need, knowing there will probably be a delay in them receiving it.

10. It is unethical to specify net charges which are exclusive of taxes or other payments which will be included in the gross cost.

11. It is unethical to sign letters with an indecipherable signature so that customers will have difficulty in tracing the writer.

12. It is unethical to act knowingly on doubtful assumptions which you purposely do not check out in case they would place you at a disadvantage.

13. It is unethical to expect subordinates to undertake tasks for your personal convenience, e.g. purchase cigarettes, instead of doing their job.

14. It is unethical always to select the more expensive items on the menu and charge them to the company when you are away from home on company business.

15. It is unethical to use a company guest as a means of satisfying a desire which you otherwise could not afford, e.g. inviting the guest to an opera you wish to see when you are asked to act as company host.

How many of the unethical practices which you disagree with do you carry out?

How many of the unethical practices which you disagree with are prevalent in the company?

11.3   IMPACT OF TECHNOLOGY

Review the effects which the impact of technology has had on your job (and that of your direct reports) over the past three to five years. List those which you believe have had a positive influence on the ethical aspects of your relationships with customers. List those which have had a negative effect on the ethical aspects of your relationships. Determine what action you must take to raise the standard of ethical relationships in terms of:

— Quality of advice;
— Charges;
— Amount of time devoted to the customer;
— Other matters (specify).

11.4   IMPACT OF LEGISLATION

Review the effects which the impact of legislation has had on your job (and that of your direct reports) over the past three to five years. List those which you believe have had a positive effect on the ethical aspects of your relationships. Determine what action you must take to raise the standard of ethical relationships in terms of:

— Compliance with legislation;
— Quality of advice on legislative matters;
— Other matters (specify).

11.5   ADVERTISING

Identify your main competitors and analyse their advertising and literature. Decide in what ways their claims or advice appear unethical – give your reasons. Discuss if, on the basis of your analysis, the competitors have higher or lower standards of ethical banking. In the light of our findings draw up recommendations to deal with the situation.

11.6 RELATIONSHIPS

Hold a one-hour discussion session in which each participant in turn makes a contribution, beginning 'I feel uncomfortable about . . .', continuing with an ethical aspect of customer or other relationship. Do not discuss or comment until every participant has made a contribution on some matter. Decide on one or two contributions which you will discuss and resolve in some way at this meeting, carrying the others forward to subsequent meetings or alternative action.

11.7–10 ETHICAL TRAPS

Review the 'ethical traps' in Table 4.1. Identify those into which you have fallen in the past. Determine to what extent you had it within your power to avoid the traps. What inhibited you from using your power?

11.8

Identify the 'ethical traps' which currently lie in wait for you. What action do you plan to avoid the traps? What help do you need? How will you get this help? What alternative action will you take if the help is not forthcoming?

11.9

What additional 'ethical traps' have you encountered in your career? If you have staff reporting to you what advice would you give them to avoid the traps?

11.10

What additional 'ethical traps' affect your company? What action can you as a group take to avoid these traps? What help do you need? How will you get the help you need?

11.11–12   CANONS OF ETHICAL BANKING

Consider the canons of ethical banking. Is there an additional canon which would apply to your company? If so, discuss the reasons for the addition, and its implications for ethical behaviour.

11.12

In your company, which of the canons will be most difficult to comply with? Discuss your reasons and draw up guidelines for compliance.

11.13   CODE OF BANKING PRACTICE

Consider the summary of the Code of Banking Practice in Chapter 6. What changes would the code make to your job? How best can you be prepared for these changes?

11.14   CUSTOMER EDUCATION

From your experience what are the main 'bank education' needs of customers? How should your company set about meeting these needs?

11.15–16   DECLINING LOANS

If required to give full reasons for declining loan applications, what changes would be necessary in the credit control policies and practices of your bank?

11.16

Draw up 'typical cases' where loan applications have been declined. Suggest guidelines for dealing with such cases in accordance with the five canons of ethical banking.

12 Ethical Problems

12.1 THE SUICIDE PROBLEM

You are the manager of a branch of Alpha Bank. One of your customers, Tom Brent, has defaulted on a loan and you have been instructed by head office to put Brent Plastics into receivership.

Tom Brent has been an 'awkward customer' in almost every sense of the words; morose, inefficient and difficult to negotiate with. You will not be sorry to see the back of him.

His wife, who has her personal account at the branch, asked to see you urgently last week. Reluctantly you agreed. She told you that Brent is a homosexual and was diagnosed two months ago as having contracted AIDS. This she says has contributed to his lack of interest in the business.

You know that their house was pledged as security for the business loan and will therefore be repossessed by the bank.

She asked you to give Brent one last chance: 'He's beside himself. He says the only thing he'll do is kill himself in a car accident or something, so I can collect on his life policy. That would cover all his debts and let me keep the house. Oh, I shouldn't have told you that. Forgive me. Please forget what I said.'

You decided you had no option but to go ahead and have a receiver appointed. You telephoned Brent to forewarn him. His wife answered and said in a distraught voice: 'It's too late, Tom was killed in a crash last night. He smashed into a lorry on the motorway. It was very foggy. Incidentally, what I told you the other day was a pack of lies to get your sympathy. Sorry.'

Would you:

(1) Express your condolences and leave matters as they are?
(2) Tell Mrs Brent that you feel you have a duty to appear at the Coroner's inquest?
(3) Phone head office and explain the whole situation and ask for guidance?
(4) Or ? ? ?

12.2 THE FOREIGN STUDENT PROBLEM

You are the manager of an Alpha Bank branch in a British university city with a large Moslem population. One of your customers is a Middle East student, Osman Habba, a member of a very rich family. For the past three years money has been no problem for Osman. His family has sent him a bank draft every month which covered his ever increasing expenses.

Two years ago, Habba was charged with the illegal possession of drugs but as his father was foreign minister of a friendly power, the case was dismissed. You have met Habba twice at the request of the Overseas Division; each time you gained the impression of a pampered, arrogant young man still indulging in drugs.

Six months ago, there was a revolution in Habba's country and all his family were executed. Their assets at home were sequestrated by the new regime, their assets abroad were frozen by the new government now recognised and courted by Britain.

Habba's funds ran out two months ago. You have asked him to see you since he has accumulated debts of over £25 000.

On entering your office Habba is as arrogant as ever, and is apparently under the influence of drugs. He tells you that since the death of his family he has been prescribed drugs for his nerves. He can see no way of paying off his debt, but he expects the bank to support him until he has completed his degree in eighteen months' time.

'After all,' he says, 'my family were long-standing customers of this bank. Besides, when the present regime is toppled I will be able to use the funds in Switzerland which are temporarily frozen. The new regime in my country is unpopular with Moslems in Britain, many of whom are customers of your bank. If it got out that you were victimising me, life could get very uncomfortable for you. So can we stop playing silly games over a trifling sum of money and agree that you give me a loan or overdraft to see me through university?'

Would you:

(1) Agree a loan overdraft for Habba?
(2) Tell him you will not agree with blackmail?
(3) Phone Overseas Division for advice?
(4) Or ? ? ?

12.3 THE HANDICAP BUSINESS PROBLEM

You are the manager of a small town branch of Alpha Bank. You had a recent audit report which criticised you for 'lack of rigour in handling problem accounts'.

Your General Manager has just issued a circular urging greater control of bad and doubtful debts: 'We have entered a period when customers, particularly those running small businesses, can no longer be given the benefit of the doubt.'

You know that if you are to have any chance of promotion you need to be more hard-hearted in dealing with customers who do not comply with lending conditions. You've asked your assistant to provide you with the five most difficult, bad and doubtful cases. Having studied the files you have resolved how to deal with three of the cases, but the remaining two are difficult; Desktop Computers and the Old Hall Riding School.

Desktop Computers needs an injection of working capital if it is to survive over the next three months. It is the main employer in the town and has attracted national attention for its employment of the disabled in assembly work. Growing competition has made business difficult, but you have been assured by the Managing Director, whom you trust, that they are on the verge of a technological breakthrough which will cut costs and 'allow us to employ more people'.

The Old Hall Riding School has been established three years. It's owner, a spinster, Miss Hogg, has developed some simple aids and riding techniques which allow autistic and handicapped children to ride ponies. Unfortunately, her work for the handicapped children has distracted her from building up a profitable clientele. The result is that she is on the verge of bankruptcy and will lose both her school and her home which are secured against her loan. You have considered a rescheduling of payments but matters have gone too far to make this practicable.

Either Desktop Computers or the Old Hall Riding School will need to close.

Would you:

(1) Draw up contrasting pros and cons in each case and decide accordingly?

(2) Apply the canons of lending rigorously and reach a purely financial decision?

(3) Seek the help of Head Office?

(4) Or ? ? ?

12.4   THE WHISTLE BLOWER'S PROBLEM

You are a manager in the Foreign Exchange Department of an international bank based in Ruritania. A radical government has been democratically elected and it threatens to nationalise all Ruritanian banks, claiming they are overmanned and exploitative. The government has rushed through legislation imposing a wide range of exchange controls.

These hastily drafted controls leave many loopholes for financial experts, but there is a so-called 'catch-all' law which states: 'No monies in any currency will be exported from Ruritania unless such action will be of clear benefit to Ruritania and its citizens.'

You have been called in by the General Manager to countersign a transfer of millions of Ruritanian dollars to a Swiss numbered account in Geneva. The General Manager says: 'Don't worry, this is in accordance with the regulations in my opinion. We've got to remember that governments change and if we don't look after ourselves now who will? Always remember if these people have their way, we will all be out of work and our families will suffer.'

Would you:

(1) Countersign without question?

(2) Question the General Manager and then sign?

(3) Inform the exchange control authorities?

(4) Or ? ? ?

12.5   THE FOREIGN BANK ENTREATY PROBLEM

You are the Direct Mail Marketing Manager of Alpha Bank. It is a job you have performed for eight years and you are bored with it.

However, you have acquired a depth of expertise in the subject which outmatches that of any other local bank. You feel that while you are being reasonably rewarded by your bank, in terms of your career, you are being held back by your expertise which could not easily be replaced.

Last month you discussed the situation with your boss who said he would see what he could do. The result was a 20 per cent salary increase and the addition of the word 'Senior' to your title. While welcoming the additional money you would have preferred promotion, but it will now be some time before you feel able to raise the matter again.

Two weeks ago you were contacted by a headhunter representing one of the fastest growing foreign banks. You have just finished dinner with the President of the foreign bank who has offered you the job of Vice-President Marketing at almost twice your current salary and with real promotion prospects. 'I'll be honest with you,' said the President, 'we are particularly interested in your knowledge of the direct mail market over here. I would want to feel we could tap that knowledge from day one.'

Would you:

(1) Accept the job on the President's terms?
(2) Tell the President you are unwilling to divulge confidential data?
(3) Discuss the situation with your current boss?
(4) Or ? ? ?

12.6 THE PROUD FAMILY PROBLEM

You are the manager of a branch of Alpha Bank. The Watson family have been customers of the bank for forty years. Once prominent footwear manufacturers, they were unable to cope with foreign competition and the business was sold to an Italian company fifteen years ago.

The proceeds of the sale went to Ivor Watson, married son of the founder. He has squandered most of the money on drinking and gambling. His wife would have left him long ago had it not been for their child Jenny. She is twenty-two and is a brilliant pianist. She just missed qualifying for a scholarship, but is halfway through a five-year course at the Royal Academy of Music.

Ivor Watson came to you to seek your help before Jenny went to the Academy. He said: 'It's no good Jenny starting this course if she can't finish it. I want to take out a second mortgage on my house for £25 000 and put it aside for Jenny's studies.'

Six months ago Mrs Watson came to see you and said that over the past two years most of the money in what she called 'Jenny's account' had gone on the gambling and drinking sprees of her husband. There was virtually no money left. Unless some arrangements could be made Jenny would have to stop her studies.

You have considered the situation and can find no way in which the bank could be of help. Mrs Watson has just phoned to say that there is a music scholarship for children of impoverished families who, despite a low income, have sacrificed and saved for their child's tuition. She asks you to agree to act as a referee and to put their case to the charity providing the scholarship.

You doubt if a comfortable middle-class home in which the father managed to squander £25 000 in a couple of years is what the charity had in mind for its beneficiaries. On the other hand, the daughter should not be victimised for the sins of her father.

Would you:

(1) Tell Mrs Watson that you cannot help?
(2) Seek to answer the charity in a way that is economical with the truth?
(3) Have a showdown with Ivor Watson, telling him it is his responsibility to look after his daughter, not yours?
(4) Or ? ? ?

12.7   THE EMBRYO RESEARCH PROBLEM

You are the manager of a branch of Alpha Bank. You are strongly opposed to research on the human embryo. A new company, Newgrotech, specialising in genetic engineering has been established in the area and has opened a number of accounts with your branch. The financial state of Newgrotech is very sound and profit projections are most encouraging.

This year the bank has introduced a profit-sharing scheme by which every employee in the branch will benefit from profit growth above a certain figure. There is an incentive to get rid of unprofitable accounts.

It is plain for all staff to see that Newgrotech is going to give the branch the profits boost that will result in them receiving a substantial bonus. Equally, they know that the least profitable account in relation to the work involved is that of St Edward's Church. To make matters worse, St Edward's is nearer another Alpha branch which, according to bank guidelines, should 'be assigned the account unless this is unacceptable to the customer'. Ironically, the same situation applies to Newgrotech, though a different branch is involved.

As Newgrotech prospers there is regular mention in the national press of its deep involvement in embryo research. This disturbs you and particularly your wife who is on the Council of the National Anti-embryo Research Group.

Matters are made worse for you by the other Alpha managers who frequently comment on your luck in having such a 'gold-mine' as a customer.

You feel that Newgrotech is becoming a source of stress. You wish you were rid of it. Last night you spoke in confidence to a retired branch manager who said: 'If we had to agree on moral grounds with everything our customers do I wonder how many customers we would have.'

You replied that what troubled you was that you have a duty to optimise profit for the branch, but you do not want to profit from embryos being killed.

'Hard luck,' said your old friend. 'Whatever you do someone is going to be upset.'

Would you:

(1) Continue to live with the situation?
(2) Seek to have the account transferred?
(3) Refuse your bonus or hand it over to the National Anti-embryo Research Group?
(4) Or ? ? ?

12.8   THE NEW LEBANESE EATS PROBLEM

You are the manager of a branch of Alpha Bank in the West End of London. A major customer is the New Lebanese Eats – a chain of restaurants throughout Britain and Europe. New Lebanese Eats is a private company whose sources of funds are from Luxembourg.

Your branch has to deal with financial arrangements for the whole group. Today, your assistant has come to you with 'something odd'. He has noticed that there are a few branches which never send money to New Lebanese Eats head office, but from time to time receive significant payments from their head office. The branches concerned are in Belfast, Frankfurt and Bologna.

'So what?' you ask. 'Each is a centre of terrorist activity. Furthermore, the Cyprus branch seems to be the most prosperous in the group. It is always sending money. Cyprus, of course, is near Lebanon and Libya.'

'I know where Cyprus is, thank you,' you reply a little testily. 'I also know if I was channelling money to terrorists I would be less obvious than your theory implies. You've seen too many James Bond films. Besides as far as the bank is concerned they are breaking no rules.'

You remember a similar scare about three years ago concerning drug money. The manager reporting it to the Security Unit was congratulated at first, but when it was found to be a false alarm he was moved sideways and his career was effectively finished.

Would you:

(1) Put the matter out of your mind?
(2) Ask your assistant to make further investigations?
(3) Contact the Security Unit?
(4) Or ? ? ?

12.9   THE LOYAL CUSTOMER PROBLEM

You are Peter Smith, the manager of a branch of Alpha Bank in the country town of Stanhope. The major employer is Grants Instruments. Ten years ago William Grant came to you for a loan of £5000 to start his business. It now has an annual turnover of £20 million and employs 300 people locally.

Despite the efforts of the Corporate Division in London to take over the Grants Instruments account, William Grant has insisted that you dealt with this affairs. This has been embarrassing, since you feel that Corporate Division suspects that it is you who has influenced William Grant to resist their blandishments.

Today, you have been summoned to head office in London to meet the General Manager of Corporate Division. He tells you that it is in your career interests to move to another post. Normally, this would mean transfer to a similar branch in another town. However, he has been so impressed with the way in which you have handled the Grant Instruments account that he wants you in three months' time to head up a new Medium Business Unit. This will mean significant promotion.

Towards the end of the interview he says, 'I'll give you a week to think it over, Peter, but this is really a chance in a lifetime. Besides, I'm afraid your Mr Grant is in for a bit of a shock. Can't go into details, but we're involved in a joint venture with a Japanese bank which, if it comes off, will put people like Grant out of business. However, that's nothing for you to worry about since if, as I hope, you accept my offer, you will be well away when Grants folds up. Besides, if Grant had been a customer of Corporate Division we would have felt differently, but he's spurned our involvement, so that's that. All the best, but do let me know your decision within a week.'

Would you:

(1) Go home and discuss the whole situation with your wife, whom you know wants to move from Stanhope?
(2) Go home and present the offer to head the Medium Business Unit as a fait accompli, without mention of the alternative of another branch or the Grants Instrument situation?
(3) Decide to accept the Medium Business Unit offer on condition you can forewarn Grant of the impending Japanese threat and try to help him get the best deal?
(4) Or ? ? ?

12.10   THE GOLF CLUB PROBLEM

Your name is Paul Williams and you are manager of a branch of
Alpha Bank. You and your wife are keen golfers. The country club is
the social centre of the area and many of your more affluent customers are fellow members. A vacancy has arisen on the club committee and you have been asked by the Chairman and Treasurer to
put your name forward with their support. They assure you that if
you do so you will be unopposed.

You are flattered and your wife is delighted. It is a clear sign that
you have been 'accepted' into what is a rather closed community. A
further cause of satisfaction is that John Robinson, manager of the
local branch of Beta Bank, Alpha's main competitor, has been a
member of the country club for some years but has, as far as you
know, never been asked to join the committee.

The chairman of Alpha Bank is on record that the prime task this
year is to win over business customers from Beta. You believe that
your club committee membership will help you extend your contacts
in a natural way with members of the club who are Beta customers.

You are in the locker room when, out of sight, you overhear John
Robinson talking to the club gossip, Philip, who says, 'I bet you feel
your eye has been put out by Williams being nominated to the
Committee.'

'Not a bit of it. If I know our Hon. Treasurer, he's in a financial
mess and wants Williams' bank to bail him out. Of course, I'm only
guessing, but as far as I'm concerned, Williams is welcome to it. Let's
have a drink.'

Would you:

(1) Leave things as they are, avoiding possible ill-feeling in raising
    the matter with the Treasurer on the basis of Robinson's specula-
    tion?
(2) Approach the Chairman and Treasurer for a discussion on club
    finances?
(3) Phone your regional boss, asking for guidance on taking on the
    committee work as an additional 'workload' although it will assist
    in marketing to Beta Bank customers?
(4) Or ? ? ?

12.11   THE CLOSE FRIEND PROBLEM

You are Bob Prince, manager of a branch of Alpha Bank. You and your wife have been close friends of George and Molly Shaw who built up a national retail chain from a local store specialising in organic foods – Green Fingers Ltd.

For ten years both families have gone on holiday together. Three years ago the Shaws bought a villa in Spain and you have greatly enjoyed your holidays there.

Green Fingers Ltd banks with the Corporate Division of Alpha Bank. You handle the personal account only of Molly Shaw. In recent months, you have noticed that the amount in her deposit account has doubled and now nears £200 000.

Your area manager is aware of your holiday arrangements and has tended to encourage the relationship, for business reasons.

Tomorrow you and your family are off to join the Shaws at their villa. You have just had a telephone call from your Area Manager: 'Bob, sorry to trouble you when you are going off on holiday, but I've had a call from Martin of the Corporate Division who handles the Green Fingers Ltd account. He feels there's something odd going on; someone might have their green fingers in the till, so to speak, ha! ha! Anything you can ferret out will be useful. Give me a ring when you get back. Have a good holiday.'

Would you:

(1) Make an excuse and cancel the holiday?
(2) Go on holiday and have a quiet word with each of the Shaws separately?
(3) Phone back your Area Manager and forewarn him that you will not spy on good friends?
(4) Or ? ? ?

12.12   THE NUNS' INVESTMENT PROBLEM

You are Marjorie Simmons, manager of a branch of Alpha Bank. One of the major accounts is for the Order of St Agnes which is an order of nuns who devote themselves to caring for handicapped children. A lay administrator, the local Catholic solicitor, has power of attorney and deals with you on behalf of the order. He recently suffered a heart attack and the Mother Superior of the order agreed that the powers of attorney be transferred temporarily to his partner, Nick Gostling.

Nick Gostling has just been to see you with the news that someone has recently bequeathed £250 000 to the order. He has instructed you to arrange through your Corporate Department for the money to be invested in Transworld Chemicals. You are somewhat surprised by this since one cause of the deformities of many children within the care of the order was a chemical manufactured some years ago by Transworld and taken by pregnant mothers who then had problem births.

You mentioned your surprise to Gostling who was annoyed and said: 'Listen, Miss Simmons, that's all water under the bridge as far as I'm concerned. I happen to have good contacts with Transworld and believe me they are about to produce a new drug which will be a winner in the fight against AIDS. In six months the nuns will double their money and they won't know where it came from. Now, I'm the customer, I've got powers of attorney, so please do as I say.'

It so happens that you have a school friend who joined the Order of St Agnes. You feel sure she and her fellow nuns would be horrified to learn that they were investing in Transworld Chemicals.

Would you:

(1) Comply with the instruction of Nick Gostling?
(2) Contact your boss and ask for advice?
(3) Get in contact with your friend to arrange for you to meet the Mother Superior?
(4) Or ? ? ?

12.13   THE SECRET PRODUCT PROBLEM

You are John Bream, manager of a branch of the Alpha Bank. Competition is hotting up nationally with Beta Bank which has a small branch in your town with an ambitious new manager. At a recent managers' conference the Chairman of Alpha said: 'Beta is the enemy we have to beat if we are to remain No. 1. The more we can pre-empt their activities the better.'

Today, you are seeing Jim Thornton who wants a business start-up loan. You have read the Thornton proposal and have a few doubts and are disinclined to sanction the loan.

When Thornton arrives you find him rather taciturn and reluctant to answer your questions as fully as you would like. Finally, he says: 'Look Mr Bream, I must be frank with you. I've been to Beta Bank and their manager told me they are launching a new product next month which will be ideal for businesses like mine. He went into a lot of details, confidentially like, though I'm sure you know what's going on. So if you can't better the deal they're offering me, don't let's waste any more time.'

This new product is news to you and would undoubtedly be of great interest to head office.

Because of his reluctance to answer your questions, you have doubts about the integrity of Thornton and have virtually decided not to grant him a loan.

Would you:

(1) Bring the meeting to a close and suggest to Thornton that he accepts the Beta offer?
(2) Try to get as much information as possible about the Beta new product by giving Thornton the impression that you want to outmatch the Beta offer?
(3) Suggest Thornton comes back tomorrow and in the meantime telephone your head office for guidance?
(4) Or ? ? ?

12.14 THE ASSISTANT MANAGER'S FRIEND PROBLEM

You are Betty Fitzpatrick, manager of a branch of Alpha Bank. You took up your post six months ago. Although you get on well with the staff, Peter Williams, the Senior Assistant Manager, resents working for a woman; he feels he should have got the Manager's job. Williams is forty-five, married with three children.

When you got home yesterday evening, your husband said: 'I

thought you told me Williams was happily married.'

'I did, why?'

'I saw him at lunchtime having a very tête-à-tête meal in the Crown with that rich widow Wilkinson, then they went off in a taxi together.'

'That's funny, he asked for time off this afternoon to attend to some family matters.'

'Smells fishy if you ask me,' said your husband.

It is the following morning and your clerk has brought you a list of 'significant transactions' from the preceding day. You note that a transfer of £50 000 has been made by Mrs Wilkinson from her deposit account and a cheque cleared for the same amount from her current account in favour of P.W. No. 1 account at the Isle of Man branch of Beta Bank.

Despite that substantial withdrawal, Patricia Wilkinson remains your most affluent personal customer with more than half a million pounds of assets deposited with your branch. You do not want to lose her business.

Your assistant has just told you that a woman has just phoned to say that Peter Williams is unwell and will not be in today.

'A woman, did she give her name?' you asked your assistant.

'No. Anyway, I'm sure it was his wife. Who else could it be?'

Would you:

(1) Telephone Williams' wife to offer help and if possible, speak to her husband?
(2) Contact Mrs Wilkinson and arrange to have lunch in the hope that you can maintain her accounts?
(3) Telephone the Personnel Department and ask for a confidential meeting with the Personnel Manager?
(4) Or ? ? ?

12.15   THE CANCER FUND PROBLEM

You are the manager of the branch of Alpha Bank which holds the account of The Cancer Fund. Although provided at a special rate the account is both profitable and prestigious.

Today you called to meet the new Treasurer of the Fund, Mr

Toomey, who is an eminent cancer specialist in Harley Street. As you got out of your car you caught sight of Edward Blue, a major personal and business customer, coming out of the cancer specialist's premises and getting into a taxi.

Last week you agreed a substantial unsecured loan to Blue. You had to put up a tough fight with Credit Control to get their approval for the loan. In granting approval, the Credit Controller wrote: 'I am approving this with reluctance since I feel that the loan should not be unsecured. However, the decision is yours and I am sure we can depend on you.'

While waiting to see the Treasurer you say to his secretary: 'I hope you don't mind me asking, but I thought I saw an old friend, Edward Blue, get into a taxi. Has he been here?'

'Yes, poor man,' said the secretary. 'Mr Toomey will see you now.'

Would you:

(1) Raise the matter of Edward Blue with Toomey?
(2) Arrange to meet Edward Blue and raise the matter with him?
(3) Do nothing and hope for the best?
(4) Or ? ? ?

12.16 THE ATM PROBLEM

You are Administrative Assistant Manager at a branch of Alpha Bank. One of your responsibilities is to stock the ATM with notes.

Recently, there have been a few occasions when Joe Hughes, the young new Branch Manager, has criticised your work and hinted that next time he will raise the matter with Head Office.

One of the innovations he has introduced is 'Star Customers'. This is intended to reward, in some small way, customers who are commercially important or very helpful.

'For example,' said Hughes at a meeting to launch the scheme, 'if a cashier paid out too much money and a customer pointed out the mistake, that would be a Star Customer. Only let me make it clear I never want that situation to happen.'

It is Monday morning and there is a customer at the enquiry desk. When you ask him, 'Can I help you?' he replies, 'Yes, I used your

ATM on Saturday and it paid out an extra £20 note. Here it is. Perhaps if banks paid more attention to efficiency and less to gimmicks, we would all be better off.'

You thank him, but are concerned that you will be blamed for the malfunctioning of the ATM. At this moment another customer, a woman, comes up to the counter and says, 'I wonder if you can help me. I used your cash machine on Saturday and I got £20 less than I asked for. Can I see the Manager and get things sorted out?'

Would you:

(1) Give the woman the £20 note to pacify her and stop her seeing the Manager?
(2) Ask her to wait, see the Manager and explain the situation?
(3) Nominate the man who returned the £20 as a 'Star Customer'?
(4) Or ? ? ?

12.17   THE UNPROFITABLE SHOP PROBLEM

You are the manager of a branch of Alpha Bank in a new shopping precinct. Two boutiques for women's clothes are in the precinct under the names El Bazaar and Delora, respectively. Both have accounts with your branch.

Recently, your General Manager at head office expressed disappointment that Beta Bank has more accounts of the precinct shops than does Alpha Bank. 'We've got few enough, so as long as those we have keep their accounts in good order, for God's sake hold on to them.'

Delora is much more successful than El Bazaar, though both keep their accounts in good order. During the six months since they opened, El Bazaar has not had sufficient turnover to pay the overheads. However, every month a payment is received from the owners in Spain to keep the account in credit.

You overheard two of your female staff talking: 'That El Bazaar is hopeless. The clothes are far too expensive and that madam who manages it is frightful. It's almost as if they don't want to sell anything.'

'Maybe it's a front for the Mafia!'

'Oh, give over, you watch too much TV.'

Would you:

(1) Let sleeping dogs lie?
(2) Raise the matter with head office and risk being laughed at?
(3) Ask the manageress of El Bazaar to lunch and try to solicit more information from her?
(4) Or ? ? ?

12.18   THE LOYAL EMPLOYEES PROBLEM

You work in the Personnel Department of an international bank. You have been asked to review the pension arrangements of an overseas subsidiary which is overmanned and in which redundancy action will be necessary if it is to meet group profit targets.

Having completed your survey you note that over 10 per cent of older employees will qualify for full pension in two years. These employees stood by the bank, when local politicians were attacking its British ownership and contemplating nationalism. Unfortunately, because of age the older employees are unable to cope with the impact of technology, thus reducing local competitiveness. Nevertheless, you strongly feel that the bank owes them a return of their loyalty.

Your boss, having read your report, says: 'Great, we can kill three birds with one stone. By making the older employees redundant we can reduce numbers, save a fortune on the pension fund, since they are not entitled to a full pension, and bring in some technologically capable people. Go ahead and draw up a detailed redundancy plan.'

Would you:

(1) Resign as a matter of principle?
(2) Ask for a transfer out of the Personnel Department?
(3) Continue with the drawing up of the redundancy plan?
(4) Or ? ? ?

12.19   THE CONFIDENTIAL INFORMATION PROBLEM

You are the manager of a branch of Alpha Bank and you are under pressure to:

— Get customers to take out life assurance policies with a new assurance subsidiary of Alpha.
— Increase your credit balances which are below target and if not improved will reduce your earnings this year.

With a son going to university and a daughter getting married you are under severe personal financial pressure; the last thing you want is a loss in earnings.

Last week you persuaded Frederick Young, a farmer who is a customer of the branch, to meet the assurance representative to discuss taking out a policy. In arranging this meeting you said to the representative: 'Don't expect too much from Young. I hardly know him, but he's only got £5000 on deposit and lives hand to mouth most of the year.'

Today, the assurance representative has telephoned you: 'Many thanks for putting me in contact with Young. I told him we needed to know all about his financial situation to devise the best policy. He was reluctant to give details but I assured him it would be in confidence. So I won't go into details, but between ourselves he's got money stashed all over the place, most of it out of sight of the tax man. Pity he's not got more on deposit with you.'

Would you:

(1) Ignore the information given you by the assurance representative?
(2) Arrange to meet Young and try to persuade him to increase his deposit with you?
(3) Try to get more specific details from Alpha Assurance on the basis of 'I'll scratch your back if you'll scratch mine'?
(4) Or ? ? ?

12.20   THE PRESSURE GROUP PROBLEM

You are the manager of Alpha branch which has the account for Beautyfax Cosmetics PLC, your biggest corporate customer, with its main factory in your town.

In recent years, there has been a growing opposition to Beautyfax by the Animal Rights Group which claims that the company uses animals for testing its products. Last month the outside of your branch was daubed with painted slogans such as: 'Animal Killers Bank'; 'The Torture Profiteers'. This has concerned you for a number of reasons:

(a) Staff were upset and now feel under threat.
(b) Beautyfax Financial Director complained about lack of confidentiality and has threatened to transfer the account to Beta Bank.
(c) A dozen personal customers closed their accounts in protest.

You had a meeting with all staff to assure them that steps were being taken by the Security Unit to safeguard them. You made it clear that the bank would not give in to blackmail. Finally, you asked all staff to put to one side their personal feelings regarding Beautyfax and get on with the job.

It is now Saturday and you are watching the television news which is reporting an Animal Rights rally in Trafalgar Square. Suddenly, you say to your wife: 'Look, see that girl over there, holding on to that young chap with the banner, I'm sure she's the new girl who joined us six months ago.'

'Really,' said your wife, 'she looks very attractive. You know I think these Animal Rights people have a point, though they go about it the wrong way. Anyway we're all entitled to fight for our opinions.'

Would you:

(1) Put the incident out of your mind? After all you only think the girl on the TV is the same as the girl on your staff.
(2) Ask the girl to see you and discuss the situation?
(3) Phone the Security Unit and ask for advice, recognising that you may be held responsible for the painted graffiti incident?
(4) Or ? ? ?

12.21   THE RIVAL'S PROBLEM

You are the manager of a department whose assistant, Helen, is very ambitious and frustrated by the lack of promotion. Your boss saw you last week just before he went off on a walking holiday in Nepal. 'When I get back we are going to have a reorganisation. It won't affect you directly, though you'll lose Helen. She is going to be our first woman Senior Manager of the Overseas Department. This is in the strictest confidence. Not a word to a soul; the Board has to give it final approval after I get back. I'm telling you so you can be thinking about who might replace Helen. Remember, not a word – you know what the Board is like for last minute changes.'

You have for some time wanted to head up the Overseas Department, but you do not want to stand in the way of Helen's promotion, so you do not make your feelings known.

Today, Helen has just been to see you. 'I've decided to leave,' she told you, 'I've been offered a better job.'

Would you:

(1) Break the confidence and tell Helen?
(2) Say nothing?
(3) Or ? ? ?

12.22   THE SECRET LOAN PROBLEM

You are a middle ranking manager of a bank which has decided to make a substantial loan to sustain the government of a notorious dictatorship where your son, a charity worker, was killed by a government-backed murder squad. The bank wants to keep the loan secret. You have come across the information by accident.

You have been to see your boss who is sympathetic, but has told you there is nothing he or you can do to stop the loan going through. He reminded you that the information is privileged.

You have five years to go before meeting your retirement date. The shock of your son's death has resulted in your wife being an invalid who needs expensive nursing. You want to make a protest against the bank's action.

Would you:

(1) Leak details of the loan to the media?
(2) Resign in protest?
(3) Or ? ? ?

12.23 THE HANDICAPPED CASHIER PROBLEM

You are the Assistant Manager of a bank branch. One of the staff, Mary, has a slight speech impediment which becomes more marked when she meets strangers. She has therefore worked in the 'back office' for the last five years and is very happy in what she is doing.

A new manager joined the branch six months ago. He has called you to his office and said: 'Mary is underemployed and overpaid for what she is doing. It's time she had a move. Besides it's bank policy that staff should rotate jobs at least annually. I know she's got a speech problem but I feel we're doing neither her nor the bank any good by keeping her in purdah. Tell her she's going on the counter as from next week. She'll get used to it. She'll need to, the old days of carrying passengers have gone.'

You 'promised' Mary some time ago that she would never go on the counter.

Would you:

(1) See Mary and persuade her to agree to the move?
(2) Contact the Personnel Department and ask them to influence your boss against the move?
(3) Or ? ? ?

Bibliography

A Handbook of Consumer Law, National Federation of Consumer Groups, 1982.
A Fresh Map of Life, Peter Laslett, George Weidenfeld & Nicolson, 1989.
After the Crash, Guy Dauncey, Marshall Morgan & Scott, 1988.
'A Question of Ethics', Ellie Winninghoff, *Entrepreneur* (USA), May 1989.
'A Time for Common Sense', Chips Keswick, *The Banker*, October 1988.
A World of Ideas, Bill Moyers, Doubleday, 1989.
Banking Operations, Audrey Davies and Martin Kearns, Pitman, 1989.
Beyond the Bottom Line, Tad Tuleja, Facts on File, 1985.
Choosing an Ethical Fund, EIRIS, 1990.
Credit and Debt in Britain, Policy Studies Institute, 1990.
'Is Business Ethics a Contradiction in Terms?', Pamela Pocock, *Personnel Management*, November 1989.
'Money Talks, Wealth Whispers', Supplement to *The Economist*, 24 June 1990.
'Mortgages to Build a Community', *The Times*, 17 March 1990.
Passion within Reason, Robert H. Frank, W.W. Norton, 1988.
Policy and Guidelines for Group Employees, Bank of Ireland, September 1988.
'Psyching Out Consumers', *Newsweek*, 27 February 1989.
Report of Review Committee on Banking Services Law, HMSO, February 1989.
Social Trends 1990, HMSO, 1990.
Strategic Management of Services in the Arab Gulf States, Sammi M. Kassem, Walter de Gruyter, 1989.
The Ethical Consumer, Issue 5, November 1989.
The New Generation, Research Report from McCann Erickson 1989.
'The Pleasure Principle', *Newsweek*, 27 February 1989.
Universal Banks: The Prototype of Successful Banks in the Integrated European Market?, Alfred Steinherr and Christian Huveneers, Centre for European Policy Studies, 1989.
'Yellow, Black, Red and Green (Japanese Banks)', *The Economist*, 17 March 1990.

Index